Fr. Ale

ABOUT CHRIST AND THE CHURCH

Translated by Fr. Alexis Vinogradov

Front Cover Illustration
courtesy collection of Pierre Apraxine

A Russian Living Room with an Icon Corner

pencil and watercolour (7x11)
by Ivan Petrovich Vol'skii (1817-1868)

Unusual of this period of interior art is the depiction of
he corner shrine with rows of icons, known as the so-called
beautiful corner', and more typical of simpler homes. No-
ice how the window light moves towards and illuminates
his sacred corner, whose images rise high on the wall, while
he little clutter of secular artifacts sits statically 'grey' in the
pposite corner.

Originally Published in Russian under the title
'*Home Conversations about Christ and the Church*'
by the Iahtsmen Agency, Moscow, 1995

ISBN No. 1-879038-29-3

Published by: Oakwood Publications
                3827 Bluff St.
                Torrance, California 90505

Other Related Books by Oakwood Publications:

Awake To Life (Alexander Men) 1996
The Biography of Alexander Men (Yves Hamant) 1995
Son of Man (Alexander Men) 1997
Place of the Heart: Introduction to Orthodox Spirituality
(Elisabeth Behr-Sigel) 1992

Cover and Layout: Victoria Graphics, Orange, California
Printed in the USA by KNI, INc., Anaheim, California

Protopresbyter Alexander MEN

About Christ and the Church

A Translation by Alexis Vinogradov

The following exerpt is from the Russian publication of the "Iahtsmen" Agency, Moscow 1995:

The materials contained in this book [the Russian publication] *are previously unpublished. They have been preserved only on casette tapes...*

This was a difficult time, when Fr Alexander Men' was under surveillance, when at any moment he could be arrested. Oblivious to this Fr Alexander continued the preaching of Christ. Conversations took place in the homes of the faithful.

The book contains only the first part of these conversations, carefully preserved and transcribed from the cassettes of his students.

TABLE OF CONTENTS

FOREWORD

(from the Russian edition)

The spiritual legacy of Father Alexander is large and varied: books, lectures, sermons, words of counsel at general confessions. In this prolific stream there is a unique rivulet: the home conversations around a table. This form derived from the very personality of Father Alexander as well as from his pastoral concerns and the temper of the times. His care of souls was marked by personal, intimate spiritual communion, and the time of persecution rendered this flexible form particularly important for preaching and spiritual direction.

From the beginning of the 1980s the KGB pressures on Father Alexander's parish in the village of Novoderevnya intensified. Frequently, he was called in for interrogation and warnings. There were interrogations and arrests of parishioners. Even the briefest opportunities for meeting with his spiritual children in the tiny office of the pastor, in the little house by the church (the "cottage," as we called it), were forbidden. Thus, the talks about Christ, the Church, the BibAle, and life and death, moved to private rooms and kitchens.

The form of the parish's infrastructure was the "gatherings." This is how we referred to the groups of Father Alexander's parishioners (mostly young people) who met weekly in private homes for communal prayer, for Bible study, and for "the union of all."[1] And this name was chosen by Father deliberately so that the criminal words "group" or "seminar" would not suddenly leak out by accident (especially near tapped phones). For the KGB these words constituted a ready criminal charge. These "gatherings" were in fact the usual means of meeting with Father outside the church.

Father Alexander maintained a full schedule of services, sacraments and blessings, charitable activity, and writing. Therefore, arrangements for the gatherings were made in advance, sometimes connecting them to church or family celebrations. Father would say, "Prepare your questions." and we prepared our questions. Father did not, however, prepare "answers" in advance. He received the questions when he arrived. Thus all these talks were spontaneous.

One of the gatherings took place at my home. Father had often been with us in my single-room flat on Garibaldi Street. My two sons were little at that time, and friends would bring their own children, too. Father would speak amid the sound of clanging cups and forks, and the cries of infants. It seemed he didn't notice. Children were all around him; he always attracted children and animals (once my cat spent a whole hour in his open briefcase on the floor). This noise was recorded, forming a background for the conversations, often so powerful as to obscure Father's voice. The texts, of course, do not exhibit this background. This is good, for there is no distraction. But unfortunately texts cannot convey his wise and kind gaze, his smile—that physically palpable wave of kindness, warmth, understanding, and truthfulness which Father projected.

Then, upon finishing a discussion, talking with someone about practical matters, confessing another, arranging a meeting—in the midst of noise, anecdotes and conversations—Father would say, "Well, my friends..." And this would mean that Father had to leave. We would part until the next gathering in church or in someone's home. We would be meeting again very soon.

— Mark Weiner

[1]An allusion to a petition of the Great Litany chanted at services.

Preface

In October of 1992 I was in Tokyo visiting the daughter of Mark Weiner (the author of the Russian Foreword to these talks). Mark had also come to visit from Moscow and brought along some of these raspy cassette tapes of these home talks of Father Men. We are all familiar with the experience of capturing a bit of juicy gossip that flies by in the midst of a noisy gathering or from the next booth in a restaurant. Better judgment tells us to "zone out," but curiosity keeps us tuned in. That's how I got trapped by Father Alexander's conversations on these tapes. Above the din of dessert spoons, tea cups, and whiny infants, his measured and intense sentences held my attention, and I wanted more.

Serendipitously, three years later, Bishop Seraphim (Sigrist) passed me the Russian book that was produced from some of the tapes. The spoons, the cups, the children were all edited out now, but that same measured voice was speaking again, and I couldn't put the book down.

When we are drawn by a writer's words, I think it is because they resonate with something we already intuit, perhaps with something we have heard and embraced or struggled with before. For me, the words of Father Alexander resonated with those of another Father Alexander. Both Alexanders, Men and Schmemann, expanded the spiritual horizons of thousands on their respective, as well as the other's continents, through sermons, lectures, publications, and radio broadcasts to Russia[1]. Both of these priest-theologians, rooted in the emergent Russian theological revival of the end of the last century, and the middle of this one, have bridged diverse political and cultural streams with the same free spirit of informed inquiry, the courage to examine history critically, to recognize and denounce falsehood and accommodation, to avoid all "reductions" (Father Schmemann's term) of the catholic faith to special interests, and always to point simply to the "one thing needed."

Teaching in an atmosphere of relative intellectual freedom, the Russian émigré theologians in the West found support, an audience for their work, and lived to see the fruits of their labors incarnate in a renewed piety. In Russia, however, unique figures like Father Alexander Men, were lonely fish running against the stream. Although he lived to see the beginnings of a spiritual renewal, Father Alexander himself describes how much of his voluminous writing was provoked simply by a void of anything intellectually stimulating and accurate in theological fields in his own Country. Where self-criticism is seen as a threat, even today, the church establishment in Russia does not openly endorse his work; and the spiritual freedom he taught is a hard-won grace enjoyed by his disciples and kindred churchmen and women, who remain after his martyrdom in 1990 to continue "to fight the good fight" for the kingdom of joy, peace, and light.

As polished as Father Men is even in these spontaneous talks, we must keep in mind that they are precisely that—conversations or talks, and not theological "works." Like a skilled painter Father Alexander glides his brush confidently yet swiftly across major historic landmarks and transformations in Christendom. It is not a sentimental journey. It involves the reader/hearer's willingness to enter this uncompromising examination, without either leaving us faltering in the camp of fatalists and pessimists or sweetly lulled by a sentimental utopianism. His talks and writings are a blessing, a gift to remind us in the West of history, that we may avoid the doom of its repetition and "cut through" the layers in order to live and rejoice in the Eternal and victorious Risen Christ!

This English translation would not have materialized as quickly as it has without the secretarial gifts of Vera Dychkewich of St.Gregory Church in Wappingers Falls, NY, to whom I give thanks.

Father Alexis Vinogradov

[1]Excerpts from these broadcasts of Father Schmemann are now being published thematically in the series, "A Celebration of Faith", by Saint Vladimir's Seminary Press, Crestwood, NY.

1

The Church and History

Attempts by historians to explain the triumph of Christianity in the ancient world are, as a rule, quite unsatisfactory. The pagan world was a world which had essentially solved its social problems. This was an unprecedented, stable, and enormous Empire. From one end to the other, across three continents, there were identical customs, laws, jurisprudence, and common languages—Latin and Greek. This Empire produced a huge literary legacy, of which today we have only a part; there were remarkable traditions, Greek, Roman, and Eastern; interesting mythologies, religious societies, secret mystery cults; people who were as engaged then in Eastern studies as those who study yoga today. Teachers from India would come with a variety of Eastern methods of perception. The natural sciences were quite developed; and from the ancient world we received mathematics, physics, and astronomy.

This was a wealthy world, not one easily astounded or shaken. Moreover, the ancient cults and special mystery societies had, by prevalent standards, a broad demographic base and means of proselytizing. From a modern perspective the Empire had a developed system of visual propaganda: cities, towns, and roads were adorned with incredible sculptures, frescoes, relief-work carvings; major events were depicted by a host of artists. The Roman theater was remarkable, rooted in the traditions of the Greek theater. Finally, there were the games and baths, much more important at that time as means for recreation and as means of communication.

In general, to conquer such a world spiritually was an extremely complex task. And when the first Christian communities appeared in Rome and other cities, it seemed they would be submerged, lacking any novel perspective, either intellectual or exotic. Even the itinerant Buddhist preachers were able to entice converts with the unusual: shaved heads, distant India, a land of fantastic creatures, etc. Christians did not appear from some strange land, and they preached within the bounds of the Roman Empire. Indeed, their faith was newly-born within this same Empire, albeit within a particularly backward province. In addition, this was a province in continual conflict with the imperial government, by which it was constantly subjugated, and which ultimately brought it to destruction in 70 A.D. Nevertheless, in the year 111, the famous Pliny, governor of one of the provinces of Asia Minor, wrote to his intimate friend, the Emperor: "these Christians have appeared on the scene, our own temples are empty, and I am investigating them." And he asks how he should deal with them, whether to plant informers, punish defectors or members, etc.

What was it that happened? There were certain groups that had the strength to overcome the power of this whole ancient rule. To identify this strength, we need only use one word. Will you say—"the Gospel?" Yes, but this is not altogether the answer. When we say, "the Gospel," we generally have in mind a book. But the Gospel book captured the world at a much later period, in the time of printing. Later, for example in nineteenth century America, Gospel translations were in such demand that individual chapters were telegraphed town to town. Now any book can be printed; we live in a publishing culture complicated by a video culture. At that time, this was obviously not the case, books were few, and literacy levels, although relatively high, could not have played as great a role.

So, when we say "Gospel," we must understand that we mean "teaching." The key word for our understanding of what transpired then is the word, "Ekklesia," "Church." The Church was victorious. It produced the Gospel. It won this battle. And plumbing more deeply, we must say that the victory was the mystery of Christ's presence among the people. This was not isolated preaching of doctrine but the real uniting of people by the power of the Spirit of God. It is in fact very difficult to unite people, if we are not simply referring to a chance event, a unique instance when some brief enthusiasm sparks them to run, make noise and shout. No, rather we mean something stable which enters to change a person for life, which accompanies him to his grave and remains with him to eternity.

The Church and Sacraments. "Sacrament" is for us a very important term for it is a symbol of the Church. The Church symbolizes Christ's presence through the Sacraments. Of course, it happens among us that people bring a child and we baptize it. This baptism is a Sacrament, but it remains a formal one. But in essence, this Sacrament is the act of the entire Church, and all the other Sacraments are acts of the Church.

What is the Church? To give a definition is difficult.

One theologian wisely commented that the old definition of a man as a creature without feathers and standing on two legs is accurate, but somehow inadequate. Thus if we define the Church as a gathering of believers, it will be true but inadequate, for there are many types of gatherings of believers. One can emphasize that the Church is a gathering of those who believe in Christ, but this will also be inadequate. This is why I won't try to enumerate the various attempts at a definition. But one thing is important to understand: if, for instance, a man wants to improve his physique, he can exercise alone; if a man wants to perfect his psychic nature, he can also exercise alone or with the aid of one teacher; it is enough. However, if a man wants to follow Christ, his path is taken together with others, which is why the term "ekklesia" appears. In Greek this word was used to designate a gathering of people. And the Church came into being as a gathering of believers, about whom the Acts of the Apostles says that this was a gathering where there was "one soul, one heart." Why? Not because these were ideal people, but because the power of God was manifest in them. Faithful to Christ's covenant, they lived their life in community.

Of course, there was always the danger of becoming a sect, some sort of club. Why is the Church not a sect? Because it is open to the whole world. The sectarian mindset closes itself from people, and a kind of distortion and collapse ensue: the whole world is considered either immersed in sin, or insufficiently worthy of these chosen ones, or already predestined by God for destruction, or a host of other things. We find this mindset even among those who consider themselves Orthodox, Baptists, or whatever. "Let the world out there go up in blue flame, that doesn't concern us!" This is the sectarian mindset. "Here we remain, the chosen ones, the saved ones." If from the outset the Church had taken this approach, it would have scarcely left that room in Zion where the Holy Spirit descended upon it and where the disciples rejoiced when their Lord came among them. And when the Holy Spirit descended upon them, instead of speaking in varied tongues, should they have said, "We're not setting foot out of here! This is where the Spirit of God dwells, so let all those outside this house perish!" This did not happen. As we know, they came out and spoke, each according to his ability.

We are, of course, curious to know how these early Christians lived. They lived in faith, hope, and love, and let us not forget "sophia"— wisdom. However banal this triad may sound, nevertheless, this is how it was.

They lived in *faith* because they gathered at the Eucharist and experienced their unity not simply as a group of friends, of one belief and one mind, but as a very special unity, established by God.

They lived in *hope*. Initially their hope took on a primitive form of expectation that at any moment the world would end. But gradually people understood that hope transcends such coarse parameters. Through hope they in fact discerned that the end had come, it has started, the apocalypse had begun in the world at the moment when Jesus of Nazareth said, "Repent, for the kingdom of God is at hand." This was the start of the apocalypse of the world. And everything which occurred from this time on—the crisis of the Christian Empire, the rise of Islam, all sorts of catastrophes—was a judgment and apocalypse and took on already a different meaning than the relatively neutral events of the rise and fall of the Empire for thousand years before Christ. "Now is the judgment of his world"— we live in an apocalyptic era and most likely will continue to live in it along with our children. It's uncertain how long it will last, perhaps even a thousand years. But in global terms the apocalyptic era is when God stands before man, here and now. Christ did not go away somewhere. He remained, and that is why each time we must decide: Are we with Him or do we remain apart from Him?

They lived also in *love*. Historians have examined the influence of Christians on their milieu. We notice that all were amazed at the relations of Christians among themselves. Tertullian reminds us of the notorious criticisms of the Christians of his day, "Of course they are all superstitious, but what women these Christians have!" The Romans had not lost their respect for solid morality, and although morality had declined, the ideal still remained. They found this ideal exemplified by Christian women. The Gospel put forth the following commandment: "by this they will know that you are my disciples, if you have love for one another ." The first Christians fulfilled this commandment.

Naturally, they were surrounded by many temptations. There was the theater, where Christians could go with their friends but where, first of all, they encountered paganism, and secondly, all sorts of obscenities which characterized the ancient theater. Christians had to decide: not to become total outsiders, yet to avoid being part the crowd. Evidently, they found a solution.

There is a text describing how Christians lived in the second and third centuries. All awoke early at sunrise and the day began. We find them at prayer, then going to work, then resting. At that time, in the larger society, we find gaming parlors—everyone is shooting dice, people are losing their shirts! What a great temptation! Should one separate from one's friends? This is not fully possible especially since there are professional ties. It was somehow necessary to preserve one's Christian dignity in the midst of this world. In short, all our contemporary problems existed then as well.

The first Christians managed to find balance without becoming a sect; without isolation from others they found a unique way. They became people who, although despised, were nonetheless enviable, and in the end others wanted to emulate them. This was the main cause of the Christianization of the Empire, for certainly the emperors were least supportive. The emperor had a different religion. Many historians consider that the emperors who accepted Christianity did so out of expediency. No, there was a far more convenient religion, and you already know what it was from books. It was Mithraism, an exceptionally popular religion, which was more suitable for the Empire, for government, and in general, for all. But Mithraism could not compete with Christianity.

Phase two: beginning with the early Middle Ages Christianity spread everywhere. Large churches were built, the Eucharist was no longer performed on dining tables, but the liturgy was transformed so that the clergy became separated from the people, eventually the familiar words became mysterious because they were now uttered in forgotten languages. The Church lost the spirit of community, which resulted in a colossal decline, great deviations, transforming the Middle Ages into a series of crises.

Two roads emerged from this situation. First, the occurence of sects. Indeed, the Reformation began not with Luther but with the Middle Ages. At that time the disciples of Peter Valdes (d.1205), Arnold of Brescia (d.1155), Wycliffe (d.1384), Savonarola (d.1498) appeared and there were very many such groups in Russia. Although persecuted, they established sects. These were exceptional people, often very churchly in their thinking, often deviating seriously from Christianity. Yet despite the enormous talent of these heroes, many of whom ended at the stake, like Hus and Savonarola, they were lacked the fullness of the Church's breath. They chose a particular path, announced that it was the only one, and rejected all others—sectarianism remained intact.

The Middle Ages found a second road: to remain within the Church, but to rejuvenate the ecclesial spirit. This was the path of monasteries, the monastic orders: people who wanted to take Christianity seriously and, finding society formally Christian but internally corrupt, left and formed their own societies—at times successfully, sometimes unsuccessfully. But each time an order was established it became a kind of church within the Church or, as we say, a state within the state. Their reforming power was enormous.

I won't get into historical details. The Reformation, Protestantism, did much to restore the communal spirit of the Church, and that is why Protestant divisions took the form of brotherhoods. Protestants developed the first communes (communal societies in the USA), the first Christian brotherhoods which held possessions in common—they ceaselessly worked at this ideal. But each time they lost their ideal becoming narrow-minded, and ultimately the spirit of sectarianism won out, and this is a sterile spirit. Is it now the solution for the Church to restore monastic orders? Some indeed attempt to do so, but in the contemporary situation it seems an outmoded approach to regard this as an all-encompassing solution.

This is why from the end of the nineteenth century in the modern Church there were attempts to return to the notion of the Church as a society of believers. To this end there appeared various Orthodox brotherhoods with assorted labels, including even temperance societies. They were marked by corporate prayer, common to the whole group, and specific work for a concrete goal. In particular, there were some remarkable societies outstanding in their care for the sick, for the destitute, etc. In the West they became quite numerous, their methodology was refined by leaders in the twentieth century. These small congregations tried to revive the spirit of brotherhood primarily through common prayer, the common meal, worship in the vernacular, and the reading of Sacred Scripture. The Scriptures, mutual aid, common prayer—these were the foundations of societies at the heart of religious revival.

We don't need to create any orders or brotherhoods, we really don't need this because we have the Church. But we always have to remember that the fullness of the Church is manifest in brotherly unity, in that which existed from the beginning: Faith, Hope, Love, and Sophia. *Faith*— I am always overjoyed when you all commune together— faith is the Word of God into which we enter ever more deeply. *Hope*— is always to look higher and ahead, not to get lost in the mundane; for we can simply become moldy, disappear into a pit of petty cares, stop living, and simply drag along. And *Love*—a word undoubtedly shock worn, but we have no need to create another. Think about it; many years will pass, various people will become part of your life, but those to whom you were connected by something spiritual will remain. This bond is extraordinary, it can't be substituted by anything else, it is eternal. We are always oriented towards temporary things, somewhat like school chums, students united in fellowship; this is good, but temporary. And only if something deeper unites us, does the bond remain. Are there mitigating factors? Of course. If you look at the epistles, you will see that the first Christians were competitive and jealous, and sinful. They were even greedy, inasmuch as everyone brought food, while some who brought more would think: "Well, this one brought nothing but he still plans to eat, so I better eat quickly." It's funny, but the Apostle Paul writes about this in total despair.

Thus, although we have standards it does not mean that we have to precisely mimic a given culture. One French atheist writer surmised that if the Apostle Paul were to walk through contemporary cities, he would probably recognize Christians only in the Baptist congregations, taking the worship of the rest for a kind of pagan rite. This may be true externally. Without question, the Baptists imitate faithfully and successfully the first Christian gatherings. They strive to exit the closed sectarian circle, they want to assimilate the Christian culture of Russia—this is a very positive stroke.

This means that in order to be a Christian in the Church, one cannot be a sectarian, while at the same time one cannot be a person who serves two masters. Here we have the classical perils of Scylla and Charybdis. Scylla is sectarianism, Orthodox or Baptist, when we say: This is all secular, we don't need any of it, it's all foreign to us, and so on. And Charybdis, full mimicry: when they are carrying on, you carry on; when they are mischievous, you indulge in mischief, out of a kind of solidarity, of course, but a very poor solidarity.

It follows that a Christian must be a friend of the heathen, but as a Christian must say: "I will follow you anywhere, but here, forgive me, I have to stop."

And one more thing: This was a consideration from the beginning, for the first words about man spoken by God are: "It is not good for man to be alone." And when

He establishes the Old Testament Church, He calls Abraham and tells him that he will be the father of many nations. This is about the People of God, a people, not individuals elected by God who go among the crowds, but about a people—a people not in the ethnic sense of the word, but in a particular spiritual sense. Because in addition to ethnic groups there is the People of God which includes a host of various ethnicities. Essentially, it is possible to call even a few persons the People of God; for when there is one congregation, it constitutes a complete Church, it has everything: it has Christ, the Sacred Scriptures and Sacraments, which are the presence of Christ. We must see this not in administrative terms, not regionally, not organizationally, not superficially, but in reality. Thus spoke the Fathers of the Church: each local church, that is, each place where the Liturgy is celebrated, is already the Church as it is in its fullness. How can I elaborate this for you? If you take a certain organism, then that part which contains a group of chromosomes is already the same organism in miniature, it contains the entire model completely.

So, briefly, here is what the early Christians looked like, what people did when the Church became subordinate to the state, and how the early Christian forms started returning to Russia and to the West.

2

There must be differences among you[1]

In the New Testament we find the words: "there must be differences among you." What does this mean? This means that Christianity is one in spirit, one at its root, one in its theandric, mystical foundation, but on other levels, human, intellectual, social—diverse.

We find the attempt to suppress this in no less a respectable institution than the unified Latin-Catholic Christian world in its attempt to establish one style of life—prayer, worship, ideology—throughout the entire Christian world. This is, of course, laudable from one point of view. It is laudable if in this external unity one can expect to find inner unity. Thus, a person arriving from the Mediterranean shores in the cold snows of Scandinavia could hear the same Latin hymns and see statues of the same saints as in his home land. But in fact, this is a profoundly artificial attempt. Its goal is benign, and its fruits were often worthwhile; as a matter of fact this is what held Europe together in the Middle Ages, in that the Church was unified organizationally. But as we know, this also led to conflicts and divisions among various Christian groups with differing lifestyles, spiritualities, and cultures: the uprising of northern tribes in the Reformation, the separation of Asiatic groups into Monophysite Nestorian churches, the estrangement of the Eastern Orthodox Church as a particular socio-cultural phenomenon which absorbed the legacy of Byzantium and a group of Slavic lands.

Not everything Slavic can be identified with Orthodoxy. Take Poland, for example. Poland is a fairly strong Slavic culture belonging to a different socio-cultural group. Now political boundaries have shifted, overlapped, and we can no longer claim that a certain country has a single style or spirit. There isn't a country possessing a single style or spirit any more, because our twentieth century is one of constant rebirths and transformations. Nevertheless, from a bird's eye view such cultural islands have remained. What is it that interests us today?

The fact that within the Orthodox Church there has always been a diversity of expressions and forms. And we shouldn't regard those forms which are unsuitable to us as something degenerate, or as mere remnants of by-gone days. We need to see each as simply one form of the same spirituality. Moreover, in this we discern the words of the New Testament, "there must be differences among you". In the encounter of different ideas and customs we more clearly discern our own positions. Having traveled to the West for the first time, with a particular religious mindset, Vladimir Soloviev used to say that he returned more Orthodox than when he left. Why? He encountered the West which he only knew from books, he met people, and discovered that in his heart, temperamentally, he still belonged to the East. And being a pioneer of ecumenism, one of the first to be sacrificed on the altar of church unity, he firmly understood his own connection to the Eastern tradition. This means that familiarity with foreign things is not fruitless.

The pre-Christian cosmology contained two poles—the dynamic and the static. The static pole had a very developed, elaborate worldview, with a vast tradition and high intellectual culture; life was considered to be established according to a permanent schema in all its forms, I might add. Either this life style is understood to die and be reborn anew, as in the East, in India or in Greek philosophy, or it simply continues immovably as with the Egyptians. Even the best minds, from the first priests of the ancient East to the philosopher Aristotle, clung to this idea. How did this thinking become so deeply rooted in mankind? It corresponds to what we see around us in nature, to the cycles of winter, summer; sunrise, sunset; and so on. The second point of view—let's call it "dynamic"—arose not as a conscious process, not as a conclusion from positive observations of nature, or from purely intellectual abstractions.

The idea of dynamism arose through revelation, it was not deduced intellectually. To us this now seems somewhat strange. When we have before us pictures of how the stars were formed, the evolution of plants, of matter, and so on, we understand that dynamism is part of nature. But prior to the Common Era, no one surmised this, even Aristotle who stood right on its threshold, one step away from evolution. Since he had examined the whole system of living things, it didn't even enter his head that the world might be in process. His world was static. There was no hint of dynamism. This means that the biblical teaching of a developing world was a revelation given by God through inspiration rather than through a kind of reflection or a deduction of facts which man already then had in hand. Coming to earth, Christ doubly reinforced the idea of dynamism, that is, He placed the notion of the Kingdom of God at the center. The world is moving towards perfection, towards fullness; the world is moving towards the time when all men will become the sons of God.

In Christ the Kingdom of God is symbolized through growth. Look how He loved parables about seeds. The seed develops, there is fermentation, everything expands and ascends, is determined by a goal. There are great religious systems, great approaches to God. God answers man: "Yes, I hear you, but I say to you that before you lies an infinite goal, you have not yet reached that which I propose to give you." This is the fundamental idea of Scripture, the notion of becoming—although the Bible contains many ideas. Contemporary thinkers call this the linear concept of development, moving forward and ascending. The secular, worldly, areligious proponents of this worldview label it the theory of progress, which appeared in the post-Renaissance era. The Communist variant of this teaching says that the world must arrive at a glorious future. Psychologically, this is quite understandable, inasmuch as from generation to generation for hundreds of years our civilization, both Russian and European, was built on Christian foundations and, therefore, believes in a glorious future. Incidentally, the science of the age of Aristotle and Plato had no basis for belief in a glorious future. And in itself, knowledge does not require belief that all will be well.

On the contrary, there are many arguments in science to show that the world will incinerate, or freeze, or disintegrate, or that mankind will be obliterated by epidemics. Not only are there no guarantees of a glorious future but, on the contrary, there is much to contradict this. Nonetheless, such a belief persists. And it is the legacy of Christianity. The philosopher Lucretius saw the world as dying. If any of you have perused his book, *The Nature o*

Things, you will remember that he said, "a global autumn approaches, the world is moving towards decline." All the pagans felt this way. And the Greek poet Hesiod, in *Works and Days*, constructs a system of ages. The first was the Golden Age, and then worse and worse—he called his own the Age of Steel. Everything approaches the natural annihilation of the world. In the past everything was better.

But Christianity affirms that the best lies ahead. And this is based on Holy Scripture. When the Gospel appeared in the ancient world, there began a process of mutual interaction. This is not strictly data, my friends, not simply history. We are now being nourished spiritually in our Church and intellectual life with the fruits of this interaction.

Church life in the era of Constantine was a period of interaction between Christianity and paganism. This interaction began earlier, already in the second century. Can this really be considered a catastrophe, a collapse, a failure of Christianity? Not in the least! Can we say that this is wonderful and great? Neither can we say this. There is no single answer. Absorbing elements of paganism into itself, Christianity in this way sanctified all that was wonderful in the legacy from India to the New World. We can say that in the course of all millennia not a single soul which strived towards God passed unnoticed by him. Not one spark of the spectacular in the whole history of art passed unnoticed within the beauty of the world.

No matter where pagan concepts originated, they always had elements adaptable to Christianity, not in a spirit of compromise or expediency, but because of their innate worthiness. If some of our hymns contain echoes of the hymns of Osiris, that only makes me happy, knowing that we have received that eternal intuition of the resurrection which the ancient Egyptian experienced on the shores of his native river. Within the surrounding lifeless desert, he suddenly saw from this clay, this earth, this silt, the rising of first shoots. He saw the sun pulling them upwards and he sang, "Osiris has conquered death by death." And we repeat those marvelous words, the Church adopts them. In the Church there were poets enough to invent something original. But this early Christian sensitivity was an act of reverence, if you will, of love and affection towards the whole non-biblical world, which we inaccurately call "pagan."

But this is not enough. There is a neutral symbolism—for example, our painted Easter eggs, our festal foods, all sorts of Western customs unfamiliar to you, but rooted in paganism. They are neutral, yet they are wonderful. Why are they wonderful? Because they are connected with matter, with the world, with nature. Christmas trees, colored eggs lying in baskets of growing grass—these things which enter one's soul from childhood are a kind of hymn of nature, related to our understanding of God's presence in the world. But these connections also had negative aspects. There were at times direct compromises. To adopt the famous words, "trampling down death by death," into a Christian hymn was not a compromise, whereas to bring into Christian life and Christian commandments laws which contradict the Church and the Gospel is dangerous. I don't propose to unravel this idea further; it has already been adequately studied by Vladimir Soloviev in his essay, "On the Decline of the Medieval Worldview." I summarize this second thesis: Seeing itself in the world, Christianity partially adopted a static model.

The third thesis is this: There is the medieval worldview which, on the one hand, still preserved the biblical tendency forward towards the Kingdom of God

Here we find the teaching of the abbot Joachim da Flora (1132-1202) on the three Testaments: the Old, the New, and the future Eternal Covenant. On the other hand, the idea of a static world gained prominence. Perhaps some of you are curious and have perused contemporary books on the Middle Ages, where this notion appears in the following form: at the top is God, below Him the angels, below them the king, surrounded by the saints, nobility—a kind of static hierarchy, that is, a heavenly hierarchy and an earthly one, joined together, one reflected in the other. A perfected and final society. A recurrence of what existed in the ancient East.

This theory applied to a society which tried to imagine that God's will had already been accomplished within it, yet people felt burdened by it. The Middle Ages are not as romantic as people now think! I always enjoyed Andersen's fable, "The Lucky Boots," about magical boots. Do you remember how a person was praising the Middle Ages, and suddenly finding himself transported to a street of that time, drowned in the mud and barely managed to get out? So, here's the scene, let's use Soviet jargon—feudal servitude blessed by the Church, a very tragic sight indeed. It must be said that some of the worst cruelties of the Inquisition were carried out by the Government. The Spanish Inquisition belonged precisely to the Crown. But then arises a frightening, pessimistic notion which runs like a red thread through the whole mindset of the Middle Ages to our present day: the idea of an unfulfilled history. God came and promised us something. He brought something unusual into the world, which cannot seem to materialize. There follows an intense apocalypticism and eschatologicism—I put it this way for the sake of brevity. You understand: the world didn't work out, it didn't succeed, and so its only salva-

31

tion is that God's judgment will destroy it all and throw it out. Out of this come revolutionary sects, movements, various Anabaptists, Old-Believers, I won't list them all, you know them. From this also comes a fairly early asceticism, not an evangelical one, but rather one which we now find under the banner of renunciation of the world.

The Gospel teaches us that the love of the Pre-eternal One for the world is so great that he gives himself, his power, so that the world may be saved. And suddenly it seems to people that the world is something horrible, that nothing remains but to inflict punishment—the fiery Gehenna—upon it. Then begins the flight from the world, starting in the fourth century, and actively developed in the Middle Ages. I am not claiming that monastic movements, modeled by the Church on pagan cults, were without purpose. They indeed had meaning, for the deepening of spiritual life, for the development of prayer and contemplative practice, for the preservation of spiritual, intellectual and theological values as well as cultural values. Monasteries were places where frescoes were painted, books published, scientific theories and accomplishments were developed and preserved. All the same, the idea that the world is fallen, wallows in sin, but we who have gathered here are saved—this notion, of course, is entirely foreign to the Gospel, completely foreign to the One who speaks of the shepherd leaving the ninety-nine sheep in order to save one. Was Christianity then not ascetical? No, of course it contributed an element of asceticism. There isn't a single answer. But if you insist on a single answer, you may do so dialectically: renunciation of the world, in order to reclaim it on another level. Those who have read books from India will readily see that it is not the world which has value because of man, but man has value for the gods, God returns everything to us in a better form

32

in other words, the transfiguration of the world. This is very evident in the personality and life of St.Francis of Assisi. He reached the limits of asceticism. He left his father, house, profession, became nothing. He lost everything. It would appear that for him the world was totally useless. And yet, there was no person in medieval hagiography who had greater love for each goat, each person, each creature, each facet of nature—he treated them as brothers and sisters. You know all this. Well, here is the fundamental evangelical attitude. Francis of Assisi preached the Gospel anew to the medieval world as an ascetic who loved the world.

In the East there lived a very famous holy man, whose name I won't mention. He didn't wash for forty years, bound himself with ropes, his body rotted, and he had an intolerable odor. But this was a political reactionary who supported particularly repressive measures against the heretics, the Jews. Emperors sought his advice. When they tried to act according to their own laws and not the Gospel, he immediately sent emissaries from his desert with appropriate instructions. Of course it is not for us to judge, but for the Gospel. It judges holiness. In the light of the Gospel it is clear that all this is unnecessary. We receive no preaching about rotten ropes and columns. A man does not become holy by simply not washing for forty years; this is the witness of Tradition.

As a result of difficult trials the Church received a great gift from heaven—and don't grin, now—this gift is *theism*, wretched atheism and the whole anti-Christian movement. Only worse things would have befallen the Church if these movements had not occurred, if there had been no atheism. I fear that then the Christian world would have indeed been suffocated by the atheists in the guise of Christians. I have in mind all sorts of Grand Inquisitors. Within the narrow bounds of his historical perspective Dostoevsky considered his description of the Grand Inquisitor a normal picture of Latin prelates. But this is an entirely international and inter-confessional category. Calvinist pastors could easily fit as well as Orthodox. This means that atheism is a gift of God. It is not at all a defeat for Christians. It is a great healing and strengthening force. Some will disagree with me saying, "Father Dmitri Dudko says otherwise." But he and I are discussing different things. He is criticizing the godless—and with good reason. I am approaching this on a higher plane.

Of course, it is bad that churches are closed. Who would say this is good? It is bad from the standpoint of the faithful as well as from the standpoint of the law. But I am convinced that not a single temple was closed without the will of God. Good things were always taken from the unworthy. The history of the Church is that of the Bible, where the covenant prevailed. "I give you life or death," says the Book of Deuteronomy, "choose your path." "And don't say 'we have the temple'," reminds Jeremiah, "I will destroy the temple, and its ark will not be remembered." It would seem that the temple is the very place of God's dwelling. He chooses it for His own mystical presence, and yet He makes it a place where jackals roam. Does this apply only to the Temple of Solomon, or to the Temple of Herod II, as well? No, this applies to any place of worship of the God of revelation. It applies to all temples. Of course, without argument, we feel sorrow over the destruction of the Cathedral of Christ the Savior[2]. On the other hand, we must admit that there was some deficiency in our Christian life which allowed this to happen. Of course, we regret that the superb Temple of Herod was destroyed. Such was the historical "karma"

That's why I feel that one of the main aims of today's Christians is not conflict with atheism. Many have fought against atheism.

I recently read an excerpt of the disputes of the 1920's. Alexander Vvedensky very craftily denounced Lunacharsky. This was a battle against atheism, an extraneous battle. What we need much more is to do battle with false Christianity inside each of us, it is much more important because atheism appears as a result of our own unworthiness. Today the Church must hear the call addressed to itself: "Physician, heal thyself." I am aware that it's easier to say, "We are good, we are the bearers of truth, while they are the bearers of lies; they are the oppressors while we are the oppressed," and so on—much easier. In addition, it's enjoyable. Do you understand? Enjoyable! The narcissistic complex is common to all, particularly to the immature. And it's enjoyable to talk about oneself, about one's group, one's community, one's church, one's people, it's enjoyable to talk about what pleases us. But all this applies to the level of immature thought, to immature spirituality. This is easily verified.

Notice what pleasure we derive in criticizing our opponent, even an ideological one: "How we bashed him!" we say to ourselves. That is so, but it does not solve our problem. My wish, my sense, is that we need to resolve our own internal problems first in order to be ready to witness before the world, because I always have the fear: give us our freedom tomorrow, bring us into the public square [it is the Brezhnev era -Russian ed.], and we'll say something so stupid we will disgrace ourselves. Better to run back to the catacombs with our heads covered. I think that our Lord God in His pity for us simply doesn't allow us to surface, because we are like nobles who do not know how to use their own wealth, we resemble that miserly ruler who was dying from poverty and hunger, while he had everything.

What is it that lies at the basis of a genuine spiritual recovery? That which is called Godmanhood. There is no such word in the New Testament but Godmanhood exists at its foundation. Christianity is the religion of the union of God and man. We are participants in God's acts. We are not simply consumers, idle observers, simpletons who need to be patronized—yet another of our typical and characteristic afflictions. We want the Church to be a mother. The infantile mind says: someone will shepherd us, someone will lead—as one learned man said to me, people even want very much to be deceived. There should be no room for this in the Church. We all bear a responsibility for her, for that treasure which is entrusted to us. On the threshold of the third millennium, the second of Russia's baptism, should we return to a medieval Christian worldview?

Some people, especially the young, are prepared today to do so. They are ready because of a mental lassitude, carelessness. They assume that in the seventeenth century things were better than now. However, I wonder how they would feel if they found themselves in some corner of that period. Right in our midst there is ignorance of the idea of Godmanhood. Take, for example, the lack of freedom. People crave a freedomless Christianity, they particularly incline towards slavery. This is horrible one encounters it daily, and we clash with it constantly People do not want freedom. The reasons are diverse, bu it's a fact. Besides this, the New Testament says, to quote the Apostle: "You are called to freedom, brethren!" Called to freedom. But people always desired something else Under the ancient cathedral domes was preserved the image of Christ Pantocrator, the giant who seems to hove

36

above the throng with his awesome glare. How little he resembles the Christ who came into the world and said: "You shall know the truth and the truth will set you free." Here he is Zeus, the thunder god, Perun, anything you want, but not Christ. The artist, of course, expresses his conception of Christ; but it's characteristic of these images that they enshrined that tendency which stifles freedom. I am not at all saying that a man should be intimate with God while disdaining piety. The one who is unfamiliar with piety will never approach God; it is an indispensable condition of the spiritual life.

Thus, we have un-freedom. We, especially the older generation, all know what lack of freedom means in practice. People, suffering from nostalgia, remind me of workers arguing on the trains: "Now, look at Stalin, there was a leader!" Many who just escaped from that era already need a boss. Human emotions and passions are understandable, but we don't need to return to that beastly world. We have the Lord, who is in no way a boss—the One who died for us and calls each one to be a participant with Him. Each one. You'll answer that this is not feasible, not everyone is active. But Scripture says each one, and thus to one or another degree, each one can find his place on this journey.

Let's move from theory to practice. Let's look at a principle, a difficult principle—openness. Openness to inner and external problems, openness to adversaries and to the world. Openness is, of course, both difficult and inconvenient. It suggests a fortification in which all the doors are open—the enemies are coming and will occupy the stronghold. But no, if the stronghold belongs to a powerful owner, he can sleep soundly, confident of his own strength.

For the present we can't move towards significant

reforms; and while these are not immediately possible, it seems that something else is already knocking at the door. You have all been spiritually and intellectually trained, not in a scholastic manner, you didn't read the dogmatic theology of Makary which was used in the past, but you have read new works, primarily of Russian religious thought. Russian religious thought flourished under the banner of freedom, openness, readiness to tackle global problems, theological problems. It was very relevant, very sober, and more daring than contemporary Western religious thought. In this regard something significant was already achieved.

Further—corporate prayer. Church services represent only one dimension of Church life. Some of my Christian acquaintances say that to be a Christian it's enough to hold a job in one place, and on Sunday to come to church and pray and then to leave and occasionally, at some set time, to come to the Sacraments. In a sense this has some basis, as a kind of source for all things. But in reality, the Church is conceived not as some sort of hall where people gather, but as a fellowship. Now, fellowship is another story, for it unites people of the most diverse characters, different temperaments, often very unsympathetic, mismatched, and far from angelic. Some of you come to church thinking that you'll hear the rustling of wings, and then it turns out that instead of wings you find an abundance of tails! That's why, as the Apostle says, we have to be ready to bear each other's burdens with great patience, otherwise, what good are we?

So—fellowship. Fellowship in prayer, fellowship in mutual aid. Someone will say, "Well, mutual aid—what business of mine is that!" Away with Tamerlane and his gang! For me Tamerlane is a reproach, like a twig in the eye. Since Tamerlane, who seems ideologically foreign to

38

us, behaved like a Christian, we, on account of our anti-Soviet snobbism (forgive me) or whatever you can call it, pervert good things to bad. We're already unable to discern the good from the bad, if only by the fact that everything is objectivized in the press. To one young man I was explaining a simple thing, the importance of effort. I told him that he would undergo a moral breakdown if he didn't work. Is it a Christian virtue to dawdle in the workplace or to be a "professional" dilettante, inept in any field!

Previously, congregations consisted of people who lived near the church. They had common concerns. Today, we all come from different places. So the parish has become a fellowship of an entirely different sort.

Concerning the possibilities of fellowship; besides the common tasks, prayer, and the knowledge of Christian truths, it is essential to know the Sacred Scriptures. For this it is entirely unnecessary to be a theologian, a specialist, a biblical scholar. Each Christian must know the Sacred Scriptures well. They can be studied together. We can study them our whole life and continually discover something completely extraordinary. If we fail to do this we will be as people who know all sorts of things with the exception of that which is most important. In the course of such a new Christian life, which looks not so much to the past as forward, new possibilities for life in the twentieth century will reveal themselves.

You realize there are bitter cold winds blowing today. The world is changing and many would like to make their faith into a warm haven, a shelter from this violent and unwelcome world. Maybe there is something providential in this. Yet, we are given faith not as an opiate, but as a life-force, the power of struggle and of hope; not as one more anesthetic. If we don't prove to Marx that for us religion is not an opiate, we'll be bad Christians. I feel that he was inspired by God to state these words, to throw us a challenge, to throw a challenge to Christians. How will we answer?

This is a brief sketch of our Christian situation. I must note that in my place Father Dmitri Dudko would be speaking of other things, Father Vsevolod Schpiller would also speak differently, and so on. Each would contribute his own particular observations. Does this mean that I don't consider their words useful, or they mine? Not at all. I will end with what I started. As Scripture says, the wisdom of God is manifold. The paths must be diverse. And if in the past the Church split apart, it split precisely because people failed to understand that diversity and unity are compatible conditions. We need to understand this now. Yes, there will be diversity, but it need not turn into antagonistic, divisive groupings, or schisms and sects. When you encounter other forms of Christianity, I urge you to patience, even if it's difficult. Confrontation is not worthwhile. Each one must attend to his calling —let God be the judge of all.

[1]The precise reference is 1Cor.11:19: "*for there must be factions among you* in order that those who are genuine among you may be recognized." Here St.Paul is admonishing the local community for divisions which foster liturgical disorder, while it is probable that Father Alexander is thinking of Paul's other texts referring to the positive and varying ministries in the Church.

[2]This famous landmark was dynamited deliberately by Stalin, and only re-built in 1995, five years after Father Alexander's death by voluntary work and donations of Russian citizens.

3

The Humanity of Jesus

The question of Jesus' human individuality seems relatively unimportant; and this explains why the disciples, seeing Christ the Savior with inner eyes, did not worry about how he might look to the people around him. However, dogmatically, theologically, this question is in fact very important because a certain approach could take us in the direction of Monophysitism, an ancient heresy that saw in Christ only the divine to the exclusion of the human. The Ecumenical Councils specifically insisted that Christ was a perfect man, perfect, not in the sense that He was an exceptional person—it is self-evident that He was a wonderful person—but thatHe was fully human. In all things except sin, He was a full human being. If we consider this within the mystery of God-manhood, which for us is so important, then can there indeed exist a person without certain clearly individual traits, without certain specific characteristics that determine his personality?

Evidently, in a direct sense we won't find such descriptions in the Gospel because the Gospel is not written as fiction, nor as a historical description. We don't find his portrait in it, we don't find his characteristics described as we are accustomed to finding them in novels or in the old authors. It is rather hard to describe him as we might find Kutuzov described in Leo Tolstoy's, *War and Peace.*

Within the Gospel we will not find a portrait of Christ such as we find more fully developed in the imagination of people who wrote about Him later on. All the same, since it is important for us, we can find within the Gospel moments which are very significant. Often these are significant because His way of life and His actions become an example and a living image for us. On the other hand, we find very dear to us His favorite ways of expression. This does not mean that we have to express ourselves the same way, but He comes closer to us when we notice His usual favorite expressions. In order not to "invent," but rather to find the more profound characteristics, requires, of course, a certain effort on our part. Here is an example for you.

It is easier to demonstrate by contrasts. Take the prophets. They walk around in unusual clothing: Elisha the prophet in a hair shirt, John the Baptist in a camel skin, also the Nazarenes do not cut their hair. All this is to say people look different. The clergy wear their special clothing, philosophers have theirs (in the old days philosophers had a certain characteristic dress—a particular short coat—and everyone could say, here comes a philosopher). It is significant that Christ did not wear something like this. We rarely find in Him that kind of special elevated pathos which the prophets had, the poets. He spoke in a very simple language, although in the Gospel as translated in the nineteenth century this is not as evident. But in fact, in the original, the speech is very plain, this is difficult to convey. What did He like? He liked hyperbole. Only He could have come up with the image of a camel and the eye of a needle! How many interpreters tried to say that this is not actually a camel but rather a hair from a camel's back, or that those were certain narrow gates which simply were named the eye of the needle and that a camel could typically not come through them. But He had in mind a normal, large camel and the truly minuscule eye of a needle, and when He says that the Pharisees were inclined to sift out a gnat and swallow an entire camel, again it was one of His favorite ways of expression. Likewise, when He spoke of a mustard seed as one of the smallest of all seeds, this is hyperbole. It is entirely unimportant whether botanically it was the smallest. What is important is that it a small seed grows up to be an enormous tree, not simply a tiny bush. You see, this is an image in contrasts.

Certain details, which upon first reading catch our attention, are also hyperboles. Let us recall the woman who was making dough. She took some yeast and a certain quantity of flour. The quantity of flour which is described can feed not only a family but a whole tribe. Why? Because she is taking a pinch of yeast and a whole pile of flour and of course there's a bit of pedagogy in order that people should remember, you see? This example stands out.

Jesus did not use standard mediocre explanations. "And ascending into heaven and descending into hell,"— this is also a very characteristic expression for Him. We can even get a sense for the manner of His life. "Getting up early in the morning before the sunrise He went to a place apart in order to pray." This means that He liked to get up early, He liked being apart. We can find several places where He wanted to be apart. However, when they came seeking Him he immediately responded. He did not say, "Oh, leave me alone." There is an old saying about one ascetic who sat atop a column and was given to contemplation. He was a great ascetic, but when his mother and relatives came to him he replied that he would have nothing to do with them because, "I have died to the world," as it is written there. We, of course, venerate this man, but in Christ we don't find anything analogous. He responds to each encounter immediately. For example, in an account in the Gospel of Mark He leaves, goes to a place apart, but then the people gather and Peter runs to Him saying, "Everyone is looking for you," and He answers, "It is for this that I have come," and Mark tells us that so many people were gathered that there was not even time to eat. This means that Jesus' life was full at all times. Graphically we can follow his journeys on a map. He got up and went, came into Samaria by foot, in a rather hot climate, covered large distances and, as you remember, there is only one place in the Gospel that says that He was overcome by the heat—the heat reached well over a hundred degrees and He sat down by a well in Samaria. This means that we cannot picture Him as did a certain French writer of the 19th century, as a frail and light person, or the way He was depicted in some sweet Catholic paintings of the last century—a particular genre of art. He went to places far away, this means He had to walk tens of kilometers. Certain authors will insist that Jesus never laughed. There is no direct text which tells us that He laughed, but there is much humor and irony in his conversation.

Incidentally we must point out that Christ created the parable form, because in the Old Testament the word "parable" meant an aphorism. The word was "mashal." We translate it as "parable," although it meant a brief thought. But a short novel, a short story was rather rare. They existed, of course, but in the Old Testament we can count them on our fingers. Christ was the first who took these

44

small novellas and transformed them into a means of describing great truths. Why? Because this was the word of life, but what kind of "word of life" can it be if we say that all peoples are equal? There is a kind of common ground. He formulates the parable of the good Samaritan and you notice that in such a story we find no moral that is directly given, or very rarely, and this is not by chance, because in the parable He creates a situation, and the hearer has to feel it internally, as we say, existentially. He has to feel this situation and find his own answer. In the parable of the good Samaritan for the question, "who is the neighbor?" Jesus does not provide an answer, He simply describes the circumstances and then asks, "Who is the neighbor?" One of the listeners answers, "The one who is merciful to him," and only then does Jesus say, "Go, and do likewise." Today in the Gospel we read the words of Christ where he is explaining the form of the parable to his disciples and He says, "To you it is shown clearly, to them in parables." Why? Because He was preparing His disciples to be preachers and He was showing them the outline, the structure on which the parable was built. But when He was speaking to the people the parable had to be conveyed without this background in order that they could find their own answer.

Incidentally, He did not declare even the mystery of His own ministry but rather asked, "Who do people say that I am? Who do you say that I am?" He always anticipated an active response from people in order that they should find their own answer. And so let us return to the irony, to the humor. I would have to say that most of the parables would have been said and heard with a certain smile. Beginning even with the smallest example when he said, "Well you can't please them in any way. John the Baptist comes, he doesn't eat, he doesn't drink, he lives in the desert and they say that he has a devil, whereas the Son of man comes, he eats, he drinks and they say that he is a glutton and a drunkard." Let's go further. When a person becomes very tired, when he can't seem to reach God, Christ presents a story, which seems to come almost from Chekhov, about a widow who pestered the judge who feared neither God or people, but who came to the defense of this widow since he realized that she would not leave him in peace.

This does not at all mean that Jesus was inferring that people should become such nuisances, He merely wanted to show the meaning of real persistence. Take another parable about a person who was supposed to receive guests: he didn't have anything and ran over to his neighbor, to his friend, who in turn replied, "I'm sleeping, I can't get up." This man continued to knock while the other thought to himself, "He's not going to let me sleep," and he got up and went to get the things for him. But why was it important to express things in this manner? Because people visualizing this picture were aroused and did not sit bored, listening to morality tales. They undoubtedly smiled. We have already ritualized this. At that time, the parables preserved their sacred character but it was an unfettered sacredness, a sacredness I would say, with a smile. And there are many parables like this, even that parable which seems to us so touching, describing the attitudes of the people of the East, was also probably heard with a certain smile. A woman lost her coins, but when she was sweeping the floor and found them she didn't simply say, "Well, thank God", and then put them away, rather, she ran to her neighbors, "Listen, look, I found my coins, I had lost them!" This is a living scene. This is well described in "Theological Works" in an essay which is called Gospel Motifs, or something similar. You see, this was part of his own life.

Now let us consider the parables which are given by other great teachers, those whose ideas are alive today in religions and in philosophies of our time. Let us take Plato's parable about the cave and the people who are sitting in it. This is a romantic and fantastic picture. The people who are prisoners in this cave are looking at a wall along which are passing shadows, and so on. You remember this parable of Plato. In this way he tried to tell us that we see reality only in its reflection. Buddhist parables are usually very fabled in which we find strange mythical creatures, totally unusual situations, almost nothing familiar, whereas the Gospel accounts all have simple subjects. The only parable which somewhat differs from this is the parable of the Rich Man and Lazarus. One of its features is the other world and the chasm between both. But this is the only parable where the Lord seems to capitalize on a prevalent theme, the only parable where He somehow uses ready material. There are similar texts in Egyptian folklore.

One of the foremost commentators on the Bible, Charles Dodd, director of the English publication "Bible" (a large publication in which 10 Protestant Churches participated), wrote that style is a reflection of a person, a certain way of speaking, and when we read the more familiar texts of the Gospel, that is, those which sound most authentic, we begin to see the One who is relating those things to us.

4

Life in the Church

What does the Holy Spirit give us in the Church? It stands to reason that those who dedicate their attention to Church mores or to mediocre things will obviously not advance in any way. They will come to such conclusions as: People go to church and they are neither better nor worse than others. Of course, such an approach benefits no one. Why? If we really want to capture at least one spark of this enormous flame, then we must focus only on the highest ideals. You will answer, but we're not capable of this, we are weak, everyone has his own problems, family situations, illnesses, particular character traits.

Out of a most untalented person God can produce a gifted one. One need only desire this, have a will aimed in this direction, and that's all. From the most useless persons it is possible to cultivate very capable ones. In order for people not to think that it's all their own doing, the Apostle Paul says: "Look, are many of you who are called wise or intelligent?"

And so it is the weak whom God has chosen. Is it possible that you and I consider ourselves intelligent and

wise because we have diplomas? And what do they really count for? It is important to preserve an inner unity
among us because this is the foundation of the Church.
"How good and beautiful it is when brothers dwell in
unity." You see a person who considers himself Orthodox, he comes to church, finds himself among strange
people, goes home and remains alone. He is in the church
a relatively short time. Whereas we come to know each
other—not on a whim or because I have decided to start
something or because you want to cheer up someone who
is alone. This is indeed a fundamental idea: "where two
or three are gathered in my name there am I in the midst
of you."

If you examine the history of the Church at the time
when the direct Apostles of Christ were active, you will
see that it was built not on bells or bell towers, not on
icons, not on glorious temples, not on elaborate altars,
not on shining vestments and not on brilliant theology. It
was built on the fellowship of people—in faith, prayer
and mutual aid.

Why do we have to constantly return to the sources
of the Church? In a way each person is purified when he
returns to the origins of his spiritual life, birth, childhood,
or spiritual infancy, the time when he took his first steps
in the spiritual life. We're always oriented by this, it is
how we always correct our path, our Christian path, our
churchly path. We correct it through the Gospel.

Church history is a somewhat melancholy study because essentially it is a description of people's sins. The
facts of Church history essentially tell us about the falling away of people from Christ, their betrayal of Him in
words and deeds. Often the history of the Church is the
history of its art, culture, philosophy, wars, conflicts, the
persecution of non-believers, and so on. But to find within

Christian history the deeper History of the Church with a capital "H," is quite a difficult art. We can compare Church History to a large river which after a flood or some catastrophe carries debris, corpses, logs. Where is the clean water? We have to direct our attention to the early evangelical apostolic Christianity. This is what the Fathers of the Church taught us.

The Fathers of the Church are its founders. They are responsible for the Church's foundation as a structure and they had two criteria: first, they always referred to the Apostles; second, they were always open to the world. The problems which concerned the world concerned them; social problems, cultural, even political problems touched them. When some people look at the Fathers of the Church, they think it is possible to return simply by mimicking them; but it is important to return not to an imitation but rather to their spirit. When certain pseudo-Orthodox say to me: "Well, you read secular literature— but you have to read the Church Fathers!", usually these persons don't read the Holy Fathers themselves. If they read them, then certainly they would know the book of St. Basil the Great, one of the wonderful Fathers of the Church after whom the Liturgy is named. He wrote a book specifically about the usefulness of reading pagan writings in one's youth. This means that Basil the Great thinks this way, while those people who invoke the Church Fathers think completely otherwise. Their attitude not only reveals a perverse way of thinking but it masks a paganism that dwells deep within each of us. Indeed, there is a paganism living within us.

Paganism is a primitive religion. Paganism is born of the human psyche—the human drive to establish a bond with prevalent mystical powers. Each one of us is a pagan. At difficult times we are always ready to have our

51

fortunes told, to forecast. If in the next room there was a fortune teller who claimed to predict the future, many would go—or might resist going on account of shame—but would love to go and learn the future. The pagan makes a pact with a mystical companion. He finds himself in a world obscured from him, and in this way tries to control the world. Somewhere deep inside our souls this aspiration is very much alive—we stand before the face of something strange, as Bloch said, "a frightening world." The Christian knocks all of this apart because he moves forward with trust. For him this frightening world does not exist, rather it is the world beneath his feet that exists. The pagan lives within us because in each one of us there are forty thousand years of paganism and only two thousand years of Christianity.

Paganism is always easier for us. Primitive religion is always easiest. It is natural to people; and often what passes for Orthodoxy or another Christian confession is simply natural religiosity which, in its own right, is a kind of opium of the people. It functions as a sort of spiritual anesthetic, it helps a person adjust to his surrounding world, over which one can hang the slogan: "Blessed is the one who believes that it is cozy in the world." Most people who find that it is cold in this world are drawn to this warmth and imagine Christianity as a kind of—well, if not a bath, then at least some sort of tepid place like a mud-bath where one can warm up.

This is all wrong! Even if I were a Moslem and came to you, having read your Christian books I would have to say to you: "Folks, it's not this way. Your religion does not consist in this at all. Your God is a consuming fire and not a warm hearth, and he is calling you to a place where all sorts of cold winds are blowing, so that what you imagine does not exist. You adapted and developed a com pletely different teaching to suit your own human needs. You transformed Christianity into a mediocre, popular religion."

Religion arises out of popular psychology (this does not mean that it belongs to peasants or laborers, but rather that it's a human phenomenon). The problem of paganism in Christianity is very complex. Why did I undertake this digression? Because I wish that when you have fellowship with each other, at least in some small measure, you would find the courage to move towards a truthful Christianity. St. Tikon of Zadonsk has such a word—he even has a book entitled, *On Authentic Christianity*. Before his there was a book by the Protestant writer Johann Arndt (it was even popular in Russia and in other countries in its time), which bore the same title. This is to say that Christianity can be authentic and it can be false. The false form is always more convenient. It always suits us better, which is why contemporary religious life is often characterized by a churchly falsehood when people prefer that which is convenient, calm and pleasant, conforms to their own ideas, consoles them, and which they enjoy.

It is not at all to this that the Lord called us when he said "the gate is narrow" and "the way is narrow." Again and again we need to understand that this Spirit is not warmth, but a fire. It is a fire.

If we will live in this fire—which will be burning secretly within us, secretly—then we will be able to go to cold places and we will not freeze. Christianity can be compared not to a warm oven but to a nuclear reactor where there are processes incomprehensible to man which somehow stimulate great achievements, that depend on his reaction.

Therefore, here is our goal—to find within us this *authentic* Christianity. Let me emphasize it again—*to find it within us.* I would be very disappointed if you were to think: "Aha, he said that we are the true Christians, but those simpletons out there are false!" and were you immediately to position yourselves on the side of the sheep, and place those disagreeing with you on the side of the goats. I deliberately emphasized that the pagan lives within us. We have to discover true Christianity within ourselves.   Here is how we can formulate what is necessary: first of all, honesty and rigor towards ourselves, so that we may together discover what our Lord wants from us, what He brought us, what we need to do on this earth during our short life. Moving in this direction, we will indeed find the true path. Let us honestly admit that also within us there is an entirely different voice which acts as a compensating mechanism to rationalize. I remember a person who was baptized a short while before I met him. He was fanatical and very impatient. Prior to this he was a very impatient Communist, after that a fascist, after that something else. He frequently adopted new causes in frustration, and finally he arrived at the Church, and I saw that he began to foam at the mouth when he spoke about the non-Orthodox and atheists. He was dishonest with himself and did not realize that in fact this awkward fanaticism was naturally in his character, his emotional make-up, in something physiological. Instead of realizing this was a fault with which he had to struggle, he raised a cross over it or—more accurately—an Orthodox eight-pointed cross, and bellowed with the same voice. The rhetoric was different but the intention remained the same. This is a glaring example of what we all suffer in one way or another and which conceals in us that divine source operating in all of us.

So here is our goal, your goal: prayer in common fellowship, understanding.

5

The Role of the Church in the Modern World

If we think of the role of the Church in the modern world, in society, in the Soviet Union, or at least in those places where most of the population is Orthodox, then we see a complex and very unsatisfactory picture. On many levels there is a deep, widespread, constantly growing hunger for spiritual values, a need for discovery, for an understanding of faith. We cannot say that there is widespread atheism among us. A deep religious ignorance or paganism is certainly predominant, but the desire for higher spiritual things has remained. The response to this desire is given by the Church because the Church is Christ's instrument, the instrument of Christianity. She is obliged to preach what Christ gives to us. She must continue His life on this earth: preaching, service, and incarnation through the mysteries. That is, her very presence must be the presence of Christ in the world.

If we ask ourselves in all honesty whether the presence of Christians reflects the presence of Christ in the world, then our answer, of course, will be negative. I am fully aware that in the heat of apologetic fervor many of us, especially neophytes, are eager to cast unbelievers in somber tones while equating the word "believer" with light. But these simplifications are possible only in the heat of such polemical rhetoric as: "black and white," "ours and theirs," "all bad and all good." I rather believe that we need to go deeper, be more serious, and to have the courage to admit that to the question posed to us by society, the Church, that is, we Christians, do not answer adequately according to those criteria which I mentioned before: preaching, witness, and presence. Probably the only thing which remains in some measure is presence, because essentially the Eucharist is not lost, although many obstacles have arisen between the faithful and the Holy Mysteries. Such is the way of history.

Even those wonderful, aesthetic, ritual forms which are so helpful to man and in which God's presence is clothed (but then, all ritual and ancient art from the time of the Old Testament were integral aspects of theophany), all the knowledge, talent, love for beauty which man assigned precisely to this—even these, speaking generously, are now rather mediocre. If we were to take a tour of Moscow churches we would find churches which were painted by amateurs of the French or German style of the last century—churches where magnificent icons hang next to completely gawdy pictures. While many churches are beginning gradually to improve externally, inside they still look pretty bad. The form of the ritual leaves a lot to be desired. In only a handful of churches can we see and hear the service in its churchly-aesthetic form.

Besides this, all sorts of popular customs which have crept into Church life are destroying the Church's aesthetic. I won't begin to list these, you know them quite well. Go to any church and they immediately strike a newcomer offensively. How did this happen, how did we arrive at such a pass? As a matter of fact this situation is characteristic of the whole East. This decline in the state of Church life is particular to Eastern Christianity. Of course, many are saying that this decline in the Church is a sort of humiliation of Christ. Indisputably, from a certain point of view this is true. There where the Church suffers or where Christians bear the burden of difficult circumstances, there Christ is humiliated.

If the blessed Saint Seraphim served with only wooden vessels and in matted vestments, then this was the humbled Christ. But in those places where the temples could be the epitome of churchly beauty but instead become all mucked up, I'm at a loss how to call this. Besides, this is not some kind of primitivism; there are, after all, bishops, people in authority, there are rubrics, books, traditions—and in these perversions we see not the humbled Christ, but simply carelessness, indifference. In general, we know where this comes from. Here we don't have the right to speak about the humbling of Christ, but we can indeed speak of how we have reduced our own faith in its external manifestations. This is characteristic of the whole Eastern Christian world. I was never in Jerusalem, but I have heard many accounts from people who were there. I saw many slides, photographs, read many books and nowhere is this decline, so utterly shameful for Christians, more evident than in Israel itself. It seems as if this pathetic path of the Church begins right there.

The most important sacred site of all Christianity is the Lord's Sepulchre, and over it stands an ugly, sad temple. Indeed, the palaces, the homes of the aristocrats and archbishops, are far more magnificent than these coarse, provincial pretensions to some sort of pseudo-style; it seems to be fated because even the recent attempts at reconstruction failed to achieve greater success. In

Nazareth they built a temple, a new one in honor of the Incarnation, and it also turned out to be an architectural failure. It appears that the East, the birthplace of our Church, is a mirror of the condition of Christianity. Moreover, there's no place where the passions of divisiveness are as intense as at the grave of our Lord; for it seems that the Devil forces Christians there into constant conflict, providing the Muslims, Jews and unbelievers a shameful picture of mutual backbiting. And so it is that we find the question which often bothers the conscience of Christians—Orthodox, Catholics, Baptists, Protestants and others: Why doesn't the Lord offer the Church easier paths? Why has she met with such little outward success over these centuries?

I myself would not put it so radically as to say that the Church has had little success. I think rather that the kingdom of God is present as always, but unfaithfulness to the commandments of God has never gone unpunished. We always find some form of retribution for transgressions. And we shouldn't think that this is some outmoded Old Testament notion. Let us remember the words of Christ speaking about Jerusalem when he said: "If only you had known about your hour of visitation ... if Sodom and Gomorrah had repented they would still be standing to this day," that is, Christ connects the fate of people, of cities and civilizations with their spiritual and moral condition. The fall of Byzantium and Alexandria, of the Russian Empire, the fall of many other Christian centers, is not only the martyrdom of Christians, but it is also the finger of God pointing to the fact that the path was somehow false, contained more evil than good; otherwise the Lord would have preserved these centers. I am speaking about the past, but my goal remains the same: to answer the question of how we have come to such a pass.

Russia is a part of the Eastern Church. She adopted Christianity from the East and carries within her all the positive and negative aspects of this form of Gospel witness. When the early centers of Apostolic Christianity were declining, then Russia developed as one of the most serious strongholds of Orthodoxy; and even now globally, she holds first place in the number of Orthodox Christians in the world. What was going on in the Russian Church?

How did it happen that this Country became the Country of such widespread atheism. I may be repeating what is clear to everyone, but I want to remind you one more time that the adoption of Christianity in Rus', which took place a thousand years ago, was an adoption of a whole complex, an entire civilization. When they accepted Christianity, the princes of Kiev also accepted the whole Byzantine tradition with the Greek language, icons, liturgical structure, and much else. We know now that in Kiev, in Rus', all the icons were inscribed in Greek. The clergy were of Greek origin. The Russian Church was a part and affiliate of the Greek Church. And having brought civilization to Kiev, Christianity immediately became particularly effective because with it came new moral values, a new style of spiritual life which, of course, could only gradually convert the people. Here the Church had to act (in this particular case I am speaking of the Church as a Christian hierarchy) as a teacher or, in Western terms, a "teaching Church." She had to function as a constant educator of the nation. Did she do this? She did, indeed.

If we study the works of S. Soloviev, of Kluchevsky, and many other historians, we will see how much work was accomplished for the enlightenment of Rus', especially during the Kievan period, by the hierarchs and especially the monasteries. But later, as you know, much of this changed because of the Tatar yoke and the rise of the Moscovite kingdom. Representatives of the hierarchy, the clergy and monasticism understood what was immediately most important for the Country—to establish unity, develop a national center, and seek liberation. A great deal of energy was consecrated to this noble, patriotic task. Metropolitan Alexei, of course, toiled to evangelize the people. He translated the New Testament into Church Slavonic, and so on; but generally this was a period of serious decline. Missionary work should have resumed anew, but this did not happen. In essence, the effort of the hierarchy consisted in the support of the Moscovite princes. Humanly speaking, this patriotic work would have justified itself in spiritual terms if, as a result of these efforts of the Church and of other social forces, the Monarchy would have been able to appreciate these efforts and in turn support the Christian Church. But the Monarchy saw Christianity as simply one of its tools of government, a means of bolstering its own power. When Patriarch Filaret crowned his own son, his son still obeyed him because he was his son; but the next monarch was already indifferent to the criticism of Patriarch Nikon.

Patriarch Nikon was a very stern and passionate man; and while he may have been mistaken in some things, all the same, we cannot deny that he did not want to let the Church become an instrument of civil power. He is accused of papism and so on, but all of this is history. What is important is that Alexei Mihailovich, having deposed the Patriarch, managed to transform the Church into an instrument of power; and this whole process, as you well know, was quite perfected by Peter the Great. From this time on, amazing changes occurred in the Russian Church. Officially and on paper the Empress (that is, Catherine) was recognized by the highest ecclesiastical authorities to be the head of the Church. The Tsar became a kind of sacred personage. He could forbid or convene a Council; that is, all the caricatures of the so called "Constantinian" period of the eighteenth to the nineteenth, and even to the twentieth centuries flourished, making a mockery of the Church's soul and transforming her into an obedient arm of the Government. All the gifted hierarchs were removed, transferred to distant provinces; and only those remained who, holding a cross in their hand, would bless the feudal Government and exalt the Monarch. Those who insisted that the name of God should be written with large letters while the name of the sovereign would be written in even larger letters in the liturgical books— those clergy remained in their places. The clergy and the hierarchs were deeply discredited in the eyes of cultured society. Cultured society had its own faults, but for us it is instructive at this point to look at the defects in the Church.

There were living forces remaining within the Church at all times. For this we have the witness of hundreds of saints, ascetics, theologians, preachers and writers. But we have to acknowledge that their lives were especially hard. When we speak about the Optina elders, we often forget that the fathers of Optina were always persecuted by archbishops, sent into exile, considered to be self-absorbed and soothsayers. We know very well that the best religious philosophers were banned during the nineteenth century, the publication of their works was forbidden.

Khomiakov, Vladimir Soloviev and Chaadaev were all censored. And whoever we might choose either from the left or from the right, whether Chaadaev or Leontiev, all were seen as being the opposition. All were out of favor because they had their own opinions, were capable of independent thought; this is the type of Church which Perov depicted rather artfully in his drawings, because he was an Orthodox person who depicted those things which offended his sensibilities. This Church was unable either to witness or indeed preach with fidelity. There was a rebirth in genuine preaching in the Russian Church only towards the end of the nineteenth century. But in the middle of the century under Filaret, only bishops preached while priests in this enormous nation of Orthodox remained timidly silent. This means that the people, who were essentially illiterate, hardly heard the Word of God explained. The social role of the Church was constantly limited, and the clergy found themselves in such a poor state that frequently in the countryside the priests lived on a par with the poorest—having many children, granted a tiny parcel of land, quite pitiable. They were stifled under the rule of their superiors, under the consistory. It is enough, for example, to read Leskov's, *The Cathedral People*, to see this.

After the democratic reforms of the 1860s a certain renaissance began with difficulty, while in the twentieth century there began to appear active personalities, some at the head of the Synod, like Metropolitan Anthony Vodkovsky, people who wanted to fight for the independence of the Church from the State. Many spoke of the necessity of liberating the Church from secular power.

Vladimir Soloviev proved that obligatory Orthodoxy is the worst enemy of the Church. When people were required to bring to work proof of having gone to Communion, when Old Believers were persecuted in the most fantastic way, when the Church was being used for entirely ulterior aims, could all this in any way be called a faithful witness? This entirely explains why in Russia there was such a rapid rise of sectarianism. It erupted during the very short period of twelve years from 1905 to 1917 with an unprecedented speed and a surprising vari ety. A terrible pall hung over Russia threatening the whole Country with sectarianism. In a famous novel by Andrei Bieliy, *The Silver Dove*, this is represented symbolically. An intellectual in search of the truth finds himself among sectarians, but prior to this we have a provincial church described where we find the priest catching flies; in fact, one scene flows from the other. When the catastrophe finally fell upon the Russian Church, then to a significant degree (although now we no longer have the right to speak this way) it was the same nemesis as when the troops of Mohammed the Second besieged the walls of Constantinople. And the Karlovtsy Synod demonstrates to what degree the higher clergy were unprepared for these changes.

Having been linked for centuries with the old civil power, the hierarchy could not detach itself, and in relation to the new power adopted one or another senseless posture: either a very uncouth ideological rejection or else an attempt to transform the new authority into a kind of boss resembling the old Czarist power (first its reformers and subsequently its successors).

I especially focused now on these dark aspects because only they can stimulate us to think and not get mired in the nostalgic glories of our Land. There is enough good said about ourselves, but we are speaking precisely about what should move us to repentance regarding the past, to repent for one another. If this were only history, all of it would look rather different. It is hard for us to repent on behalf of the ancient peoples who lived many thousands of years ago. No one feels responsible for the sins of the Egyptian Pharaoh or even for those of Joshua, the son of Nun. All of this is immeasurably distant from us not only chronologically but also on a religious plane, morally and humanly. But when we consider what took place at the beginning of the twentieth century, in the sixteenth and nineteenth centuries, we find essentially the same civilization we have today. We still find ourselves attached to the writers who wrote then, the artists who created then, the ideas, philosophical or political, which dominated then. All the forces which are now present in Russia were in their infancy then. With good reason Saltikoff-Shchedrin so powerfully prophesied the future, he already saw it so well in his time.

One well-known contemporary writer once posed this question to a capable journalist: "How is it that Russia, an Orthodox country, became a land of overwhelming atheism?" He answered in the following way: The Church did not accomplish the role assigned to her by God—preaching, witness, presence. And now, if we are to speak of the future, let us pose this question to ourselves : "What does God require of us in the remaining time, which we, that is the Church, should focus our attention on precisely now, in these days?"

Preaching. This means we have to find a common language with the people of our time, not identifying with them completely, yet not isolating ourselves from them behind an archaic wall. We have to state anew, almost as if for the first time, all those questions which are placed before us by the Gospel.

Witness. This means that we still have to determine—if we have not yet determined—our life's goal, to find our place in life, our place not in the usual sense of the word, but in our relationship to all of life's problems.

And finally, *Presence*. This means we must learn how to pray at all times and deepen our experience of the Mysteries, so that our witness may not be a witness about ideology but of the living presence of God in us.

It seems to me that the problems of the future can be

entirely approached from these three points. Of course, one can ask: "How should the Church react to the social problems of our time, and so on." I can only affirm that altogether this is not what is specifically required of us. We need only respond to these three points. We should notice that, while the ancient prophets often spoke about the political problems of their time, Christ never spoke about them. He spoke about those things which concern all times. So we too, must be simultaneously connected to our time and not to fully belong to it. This question of "what you will do for modern society," is asked equally by the conformist or dissident, the active person or escapist. We will answer all the same way: If we witness to Christ and the Gospel, if we live in His Spirit, then in some measure we will participate in what He envisaged, and His aim was never to abandon this earth. He accomplishes this even without man, but He desires that it be accomplished with the participation of man. This means that we will act together with Him. And it follows, that then everything else necessary will take place. Through such an approach, each culture will be the beneficiary only of good.

6

The Paschal Mystery of the Church

From the very outset, the coming of Christ represents the fulfillment of hope. From the very beginning the Gospel story means victory arising out of catastrophe. Disappointment, defeat, despair, confusion—and all of a sudden, an unexpected display of the miraculous power of God.

This is where we find the amazing uniqueness of Christianity and the earthly life of Jesus himself in contrast to all other sacred events and stories in the world. Everything seemed to be moving towards a certain zenith and then suddenly—tragedy and catastrophe so unbearable that his disciples abandoned him and ran away: one betrayed him and left, the others did not want to help him. From the very outset the Church was oppressed; and the Roman historian Tacitus, one of the first non-Christians to describe the beginnings of Christianity, wrote that the founder of this "superstition" was someone called Christ who was crucified under Pontius Pilate but that the superstition, temporarily squelched, still managed to surface.

Christianity was the same doctrine that had supposedly been extinguished in its infancy but was reborn, resurrected. More precisely—I'm not speaking here about Christianity but rather about Christ—the two are inseparable. For as a man who appeared in this world, he entered it with the risk of experiencing the worst. Practically, this risk was inevitable because the world is such that it turns against the good with all of its destructive power. This is why the Incarnation implied at the same time almost certainly the suffering, the Passion of God. Christ not only repeated the fate of persecuted prophets, but himself descended to the very abyss, the very Hell of humiliation, to such an extent that it seemed His aims were completely crushed.

He was not supported by the religious rulers, He did not have many followers. Those whom He did have turned out to be rather weak, frail, and confused. Everything turned against Christ and, when led to Golgotha, He was abandoned by all. It was the worst possible defeat one can imagine. Not only were there no followers, but even the women walked afar off, the women who had earlier been close to Him. The Evangelist speaks about this directly. They followed from afar; they followed Him, yet there was no one close by except for Simon of Cyrene who carried the cross.

But next to Him were the self-righteous higher clergy dumb executioners who couldn't have cared less, who were dividing up his clothes. Indeed one could have said that the newly-sprouted movement had been choked a its roots. A year, or perhaps three years—this is a rela tively short time in which to establish a world religior We know that Buddha preached until a ripe old age an that he traveled many roads. Christ passed through lik lightning, a brief flash on the horizon of history, a youn man not having received support or sanction. In this wa

His historical humiliation was total, as total as His sudden defeat. One can say that Christianity is the religion of death instantly transformed into life, and in the words of the Apostle Paul about himself and the Church one was able to see to what extent the life of Christ was fulfilled in the life of His disciples: "they counted us as dead, but lo we are alive". These words spoken by the apostle then, have resonated for all time. Throughout the Church's history there were incredible disappointments and it often seemed that she was crushed, but by the power of God she resurrected as many times as were victorious her enemies, both external and internal.

It seems that the Church had far fewer external enemies than she had within. When you read the Epistles of the Apostle Paul, you see that the Church was torn from within by passions, arguments, divisions, troubles within the communities so that quite often the Apostle himself was greatly disappointed. It is noteworthy that when he died and a certain time had passed, the Apostle was forgotten; and in those cities in which he had founded churches, he was no longer remembered and the Church disappeared. Many of the towns in which Paul founded the first communities subsequently contributed nothing to Christianity. Essentially, his preaching took place in Greece, yet early Christianity did not produce any significant centers in Greece. The Apostle Paul did not preach in Egypt, yet there Christianity flourished more intensely. We know that the most significant centers of the Church in the Apostolic Age were those of Alexandria in Egypt, Antioch, Jerusalem (this last city enjoyed a special honor); whereas in Asia Minor, where the Apostle Paul invested all his energies, where the Apostle John worked with such intensity, the Church seemed to flourish the least. However, it's true that later she again resurrected there. And from these ashes came new teachers of the Church: from Cappadocia, whose inhabitants were considered of the lowest order (it was said that when a snake bit a Cappadocian, the snake died), there appeared such great teachers as Basil the Great, Gregory of Nyssa, and others. Later, Asia Minor became the scene of many spiritual movements. Christianity was constantly resurrecting.

As Christianity waned in the Greek lands, it immediately bore fruits in the Slavic lands. When the Roman Empire was suddenly destroyed by barbarians, then the word of the Church began to penetrate precisely into this barbarian milieu; when the most precious legacy of the Roman Empire—the law, the juridical code—was destroyed by the influx of the Huns and Goths, the Roman Church preserved this jurisprudence, became a bulwark amidst these turbulent waters, the bearer of Roman law, the Roman concept of unity and order. When the Church was besieged by heretics, there were moments when it seemed that everything would fall apart. In the beginning of the fourth century, when Arius came on the scene, almost all the bishops went over to the side of the Arians. Only the lonely deacon Athanasius stayed on the side of Orthodoxy; yet again, after some time, we see Orthodoxy victorious.

After this, a new and fatal danger threatened Christianity—the Emperors became Christian. For us perhaps it is clear that this was fatal, but for the people of the time it didn't appear this way. I remember how after the Second World War people avidly rejoiced at the opening o new churches. I imagine that it was with the same zea that Christians of the Roman Empire embraced the deci sions of Constantine. But what was fatal was tha Constantine did not grant freedom of religion but gav the Church official status as the state religion. More pre cisely, he may have first granted freedom of religion, but gradually everything moved toward the state religion which was eventually consolidated by other emperors and his own successors. Thus began the secularization of the Church. If before, being a Christian meant suffering discrimination, danger, enduring hardship in one's life, then now, in order to gain admission to the royal court, one *had* to be a Christian, even an ardent one; and people chasing after honors, pensions, seeking the favors of the Emperor, began getting baptized, attending Church, contributing to the construction of basilicas, erecting altars over relics, and so forth.

It seemed that given such conditions the pagans would gain victory, that the Church would be crushed under the weight of its own structures. It is precisely here that in the Church appear fighters against its secularization: the relentless Jerome with his bilious criticisms of even the Roman Empire; John Chrysostom, a monk at the altar of the Byzantine patriarchs. And these fighters, often dying in an unequal battle, put a brake on this movement, saving within the Church that one vessel which alone bears healthy blood. Those unable to fight left for the desert. The monastic movement became an ark saving the Church's soul at the moment that it was drowning under secular power. Then came the iconoclast emperors, the caesaro-papist emperors who tried to stifle the Church.

There were many instances when one could fully expect the end, and yet each time God sent his prophets and saved his people, and finally we came to the threshold of the new medieval world. Here the processes were very complex and interesting.

A new historical moment had arrived: The transition from the fifteenth to the sixteenth century. Confident of popular support, the hierarchs became self-asured, but the Church powers did not understand that the people were entering into a new phase of development. Only isolated representatives of the clergy, the monks, Savonarola, Jan Hus, Meister Eckhart, St. Sergius of Radonezh, and others who were renewing the Church, understood clearly that a new era was coming. On the whole the hierarchs "did not recognize the hour of God's coming," they did not understand that the world was entering a new era, the opening of a new drama, a catastrophe, the submerging of Christianity into a pagan renaissance when paganism becomes more attractive than Christianity.

Once again, unexpectedly, God did not allow the Church to die. In the West He inspired a reforming movement which, despite all of its peculiarities, played an essential role, gave rebirth to the spirit and the force of faith. The East also witnessed new and serious discoveries, yet once again dark times reappeared. The seventeenth and eighteenth centuries—when worldly knowledge took precedence and was glorified, when instead of the spiritual, people searched for the material foundations of the world, sought formulas for the world—machines, this became the affliction of thinkers as well as of the broader masses. All the same, on the background of materialism, enlightenment, secularism and revolutions, the Church slowly began to find new sources of life. St. Seraphim of Sarov in Russia and his contemporary the Curé D'Ars in France simultaneously discovered these sources, a new life began to breathe.

Speaking in a certain house in Paris Voltaire used to say that in a hundred years the Bible will be found only at antique dealers as a reminder of the stupidity of previous generations. One hundred years passed, and by the irony of fate it is precisely in this building that the Inter national Bible Society was founded which promulgated the Bible in hundreds and thousands of copies throughout the world. At the time when this Society was founded, the German poet Heinrich Heine wrote: "listen to the voice of the organ, these are the last gasps of a dying Catholicism." Incidentally, many have already forgotten about that poet and his "dying gasps of Catholicism," but the Western Church lives and functions with such determination and direction that it is not afraid to steer her ship through the narrowest channels, to bring it next to the sharpest stones causing great vibrations of the ship. Only a ship steered by a confident helmsman is capable of passing through such waters.

Everyone thought that the first Vatican Council would finally embarrass the Western Church in the eyes of the whole world. And indeed the word "Catholicism" at the time of Bismarck was considered an epithet, denoting ultramontanism, that is, superstition. Ultramontanism means faith in a Pope who lives beyond the mountains; and precisely after this, when Pius V wrote his encyclical in which he showed himself to be an obscurantist and a person ignorant of the spirit of the time, God sent to the Catholic Church Popes such as Leo XIII, Pius X, Pius the XI, who quickly returned to her the authority she had had in the Middle Ages.

From the eighteenth century the Orthodox Church found herself under the oppression of an autocratic government which did everything in its power to dissolve this Church, humiliate it, turn it into a kind of pet, or finally poison it. The Emperor declared himself the head of the Church. Catherine II wrote that henceforth she is the head of the Church. The priests became the paid employees of the state. The confidentiality of Confession was broken. Clergy were required to report what was said in

Confession if it concerned the government. Children of the clergy were prevented from entering any academic institutions except seminary. Faith was destroyed because it was instilled by force. In the nineteenth century among aristocratic Russians this evoked a particular resentment toward the Church, for example with Leo Tolstoy. Only the most refined people like Dostoevsky were able to see, to decipher beneath these ruins the deeper spirit of the Church, find the light within her. Added to this, the civil rulers, who for a time maintained the outward forms of Christianity, eventually cast them aside, appeared completely in secular garb and openly declared war on the Church [*one has in mind here the Soviet State—remark of the Russian editor*]. The Church should have simply died because she had been tortured for the longest time, just as Christ died quickly on the cross (even Pilate was surprised) because he had been scourged and tortured beforehand.

The weight of the centuries-old humiliation of the Church should have crushed her, she should have crumbled. All the same, when everything was desecrated, spat upon, scorned—I remember the publications of that time with their blasphemous caricatures drawn by people who had earlier attended the churches and had been faithful. They trampled on the holy things with sadistic pleasure as only those people who had at one time communed with the sacred can. Such artists, for example Moore and others, were doing unimaginable things. We only need to remember the carnivals which were performed in Church vestments, when actors danced on the stage wearing phelonions and miters (eventually this was forbidden) There were times described even in our own literature when people would walk along the streets singing blasphemous songs with censers filled with manure and skat ing in miters—all of this could not but gradually destroy the Church. In addition, the desire on the part of zealous clergy to reform the Church led to renovationism with its grotesque forms and rituals. The conflicts among Church jurisdictions (the Russian Church split into many warring factions) informing on each other, completely undermined her authority. Inside, everything was falling apart; outside, everything was already destroyed; all teaching institutions were closed and eventually almost all churches were closed; the Church was expelled from schools, there were no books, no teaching; there was no publishing of Sacred Scripture and religious literature; all active preaching was strictly forbidden. The earth was scorched, the grave was ready, the stone was sealed and the guard was set.

But remarkably the Church again came to life. I remember how this occurred after the Second World War, when there were only one hundred churches on the whole territory of the Soviet Union. But as soon as they permitted the opening of churches they immediately received requests from twenty-five thousand communities. I remember the amazing crowds which piled into the Yelokhovsky Cathedral, and the Trinity/St. Sergius Lavra which at that time housed some sort of schools and residences. They opened one church, and the whole square was jammed with people. People were streaming towards God even though the hierarchs and clergy at that time, were unable to give them anything; neither educated clergy nor skilled bishops were available. There were simply open churches where the Liturgy took place.

The West had its own dangers: practical materialism, the race for affluence, noise, activity and an agitated society. You can imagine all this for yourself if you see the posthumous film of M. Rhom called, "And Still I Believe"

(I think that is what it was called). This mad culture is also a great danger, but it seems that especially where civilizations tend to flourish, all sorts of new movements appear: Catholic charismatics, The Children of God Movement, Disciples of Christ, The Jesus Revolution—the constant appearance of the roots of a new spirituality. Each time that the grave seems to be closed, sealed, there is a new eruption and once more the angel asks: "Why do you seek him among the dead, he is Risen, he is not here."

We all prepared ourselves for this day of Pascha to the measure of our abilities; we prepared with fasting, with prayer, with reading. In general we tried to use this time to deepen our spiritual life. Unfortunately, as often happens, once the feast arrives our energies dwindle and then we seem to slide inexorably backwards.

But we must not forget that Pascha is not an end but only a beginning, the start of a call: the Lord calls his disciples afterwards. The feast of Pentecost approaches, the feast of the Spirit of God, Whom he sends upon each one of us. This means that we have to prepare for this day of Pentecost no less seriously. If during this time there are no strict rules of food and so forth, then now we at least ought to have equally, if not more, intensive prayers, readings, exercises, common gatherings to prepare for the feast of Pentecost.

7

The Authority of the Church

When we speak of the authority which the Lord gave to the Church we must first of all totally exclude from our thinking the idea that this authority in any way resembles earthly authority. For the moment, let us overlook the fact that during the Middle Ages Church authorities often mimicked the secular powers. They ruled like barons, princes, emperors, dictators, presidents. In reality, the Church's authority is of an entirely different order. There is nothing to compare with it.

The Lord says, "he who wishes to be first must first become the servant of all." "Do not be called masters, teachers, fathers; do not rule over others." This means that at the very foundation he rejects any social power of the Church.

"He will be the servant of all"—therefore even the Pope of Rome is required to bear in his title the expression, "Servant of the servants of God," thus, albeit formally, he must nonetheless be the servant of all. This means that this saying is essential, *a priori*. If church authority must not be despotic, tyrannical, or administrative, historically it appears that that is precisely what it

77

became. But the ideal always remained and in its name there was a constant renewal, it seemed always to shine through. Any deviation was precisely only a deviation, and we have criteria by which this can be measured.

Why was Peter given a particular place? First of all, the Apostles were selected from among people of low social class, and we have good reason to believe that this was done deliberately. Later came Paul and other influential people, people of learning; and later came people of power. Already at the time of the Apostle Paul in the city of Corinth, the civil treasurer was a Christian person whose name was inscribed on some of the monuments found in Corinth; he has a place in the Epistles. This showed that the Lord first chose people who were not part of the establishment, who did not enjoy any social privilege and honors, who held no worldly places of importance, unlettered and simple, as we read in the Epistles. All the same, it seems that the tax collector Matthew enjoyed greater authority. He was evidently more literate than the rest. Also the young John who was close to the high priest, was obviously not a simple fisherman, and also a person of a certain stature.

Peter is given a special place. In this lies the mystery of his soul, for the Lord says to him: "You are blessed, Simon... this was revealed to you not by human flesh and blood but by the Father who is in heaven." When, in Jesus, Peter recognized the Messiah, this was a revelation. The fact that Peter holds the first place—this is free election. We cannot consider that it was conditioned by factors known to us. God chose an unlettered and simple man and placed him first, in order that it would be clear that the Church is established not on the energies, talents, intellectual skills and other qualities of the first teacher, but rather by the grace of the Holy Spirit of God.

Confucius, from the very inception of his preaching, tried to find a ruler-patron because he understood that it is important to be grounded in some real civil power; Buddha himself was a prince. Plato also tried to find a political ally.

Christ promises no political support to His disciples. Politically they are of no significance, economically they are worthless; and this is precisely why the power of God was shown in them. He built the Church on the faith of ordinary people so that no one, not even the least person on earth, could say, "But of course they can do it, they're Apostles." No, these are people who are neither rich, nor influential, nor knowledgeable, nor particularly wise. This does not at all mean that in order to be a Christian one has to be a fool. The Learned ones appeared in time as did the Apostle Paul; but in the beginning we specifically have these people in order that no one could later point to his poverty, to his low social status and say, "Well this is not possible for me." In fact, everything began with the model of Christ's own life, which was not extraordinary. You know what it means when someone says that a certain yogi inhales ten times in the course of a day and eats only a small morsel of rice. This may be wonderful, but immediately it moves them outside the framework of normal human standards. People will say, "This is great but it's not for me." No one can say about Jesus: "This is not for me." John the Baptist came, an ascetic, a faster, and people said about him that he had a demon. Jesus came eating and drinking and people objected to him also, but Christ precisely emphasized the fact that he led a normal style of life. This does not remove all our questions. The main question still remains. The Church, the family which Jesus founded on earth, as it grows, invariably takes on a social form. This is naturally the community; but in

79

a social unit, as in any organism, there is the differentiation of certain functional elements, and the Apostle Paul applies a biological analogy. He says that as the body has various organs and the organs have various functions, so too in the Church. Are all apostles, are all teachers, are all healers, do all share the gift of tongues? In order for this type of society to exist it must be structured. It must have differentiation within it, and by the measure of its growth there must be a differentiation in the institutions of the Church.

Before such a structure is found, we see a certain mystery: when we celebrants teach the real Gospel word, then this word is not ours but it is his: "Whoever hears you hears Me." Understandably, there is a distinction: If it doesn't matter what pops into my head, what I might say, then, of course, this affirmation doesn't hold. But if our service corresponds—and we always can know and feel to what measure it does to the Gospel—then it is so because in some measure Christ Himself bequeaths it to us, in order that through all this, through us all, this would exist. Christ wants to effect something in this world, He says: I continue to remain and I will act. Yes, He will indeed act, but through us. It follows that we share in the authority of the servants of God, the servants of Christ, of priests; as the apostle Peter says: "You are a royal priesthood, a chosen people." This means that we are all consecrated to God; furthermore, there are functional distinctions within the ecclesial organism.

Now there is the question: Why the saying, "you will bind and loose." This is an ancient saying referring to rules and commandments. Of course, here we can raise the natural question: What if there is some rule which does not correspond to the Gospel? It automatically loses its power, its inner sanctity, because it is no longer the word of Christ spoken through the pastor or archpastor, whomever. Then it becomes only their words. Nevertheless the Word must remain alive through people. It is not enough to have only books since there is—and each of you knows this—a particular power which transmits the Word from soul to soul. The Gospel book has its advantages, but a book also has its minuses because there are things which cannot be conveyed with only letters. Remember that Jesus did not write anything, he did not write in order that the letter would not be worshipped; he did not establish a precisely regulated Church organization which is why the Catholics, Orthodox and Protestants still argue about how to organize the Church.

The Catholics insist that it must be built as a single organism with one pastor at the head; the Orthodox say that each nation must have its own patriarch; the Protestants take this even further. For them each local community can be more or less a separate entity. But Christ did not leave instructions about this to avoid canonizing the rule and evolving a cult of such a structure, since it has a human side. Even Sacred Scripture was not confirmed by him. In the beginning of Jesus Christ Superstar, the disciples sing, "the time will come when we will write the Gospels;" this is a parody! In the Holy Scriptures you will not find words where Jesus says to his disciples, "Go and write the Gospels." No, no, rather he says, "Go and teach," which does not at all mean "write;" "and do this in remembrance of me"—that is, perform the Eucharist, that's all! He left no other commandments. "and that among you it would not be so," as with the gentiles where kings rule over them; "among you let each one be the servant."

Everything else developed in a natural process, and the Gospel became necessary for us—through it the Spirit of God was acting, and all the other things were neces-

81

sary as well. But naturally, in the process of history they were infected with the traditions of the elders. This most dangerous enemy—the traditions of the elders. Our Lord criticized very little, but he criticized the traditions of the elders and the Pharisees; and this is why the Church always finds herself in the state of Holy Week: she is always dying and always resurrecting anew, and the whole history of the Church goes this way. Human inventions bury her, the lids fall crashing on the grave, then the grave bursts open and the Church arises again and again. The Czechoslovak Marxist historian Zdenek Ne'edli used to say "the revolutionary poison of the Gospels always had force in the Middle Ages and during the present age." Of course, he developed this idea on a social plane, but it is true even beyond social categories. This is why the reforming tendencies within the Church, which were often rather extreme and veered far to the left, were nevertheless always justified, for the saying of John Chrysostom remains true: "the Church is eternally renewed." When we say we are the Church of Tradition then this can be even understood in a perverted way, that we are the Church which died, the Church which stopped and froze like a mummy. But no! This is the Church which revives the spirit given to her from the beginning.

As concerns the question of Peter's preeminence among the Apostles, this problem belongs to the area of faith. If the Catholics believe God acts through the Vicar of Peter, then let it be. This is impossible to prove historically or scientifically. And if in our polemics against the Catholic structures we begin to posit the notion that previously such a power did not exist, then the Protestant can rebound with our own argument and say: "Previously there was no sacrament of marriage, there were no icons, there was none of this. So what does this mean? Let's go

82

rid of them and much else!"

The late Patriarch Sergius used to say that the Church progressed from pluralism towards unity. Initially communities were loosely scattered, then they joined together, then came the episcopal sees, metropolitans, then came the patriarchates, and quite clearly all of this implied centralization. Structurally, the Church was one step away from becoming a state organization. But in His wisdom, God did not allow it. He took advantage of human sins, the divisions between the Latins and the Greeks, in order to preserve pluralism at least on two poles of the Roman Empire, from which evolved two types of piety and now even a third. In fact, there are several types of Christianity. There ought to be a least four, since traditionally there are four human character types, and digressing with a little parody we can say that the Protestants are the cholerics, that the Orthodox are the phlegmatics, or more accurately the melancholics, and that the Catholics are the sanguine, and so forth. This is a very crude characterization; but if you look closely you will see that one person who by various signs is considered Orthodox may, in his heart, be a complete Baptist; and on the other hand there are Baptists who are Orthodox in spirit. I know a Jew who, if you take the hat off his head and put something else on him, is veritably an Orthodox person—these are simply human types.

Thus the question arises (and we always come back to the basic one), why did the Lord establish this authority? But this authority doesn't exist. The achievement of A. S. Khomiakov is that, despite his leftist tendencies, he nevertheless demonstrated that the Church does not have an external authority. He himself deviated by losing the feel for the concrete, he forgot that the Church is a community of people. But any organism requires a specific order, otherwise every one will be pulling the oars in different directions as with the tale of the proverbial swan, crab and pike. But we must always remember that discipline is not divine but conventional, conditional. We submit to it for the sake of free obedience in order to preserve the structure of the Church as a community. One person does not approve of something, another does not like something else, one does not like iconography, another one does not care for realistic art. We must move towards one another. But in essence, Khomiakov was right: the Church must not have any external authority, only spiritual. We freely receive the authority of the Gospel, the authority of Christ. This is not an external authority, it is the bearer of the highest truth, which does not oppresse us but which we have received freely, opening ourselves to its flow. This is not easy to express and Khomiakov toiled over it a long time, as did Chaadaev. Still Khomiakov's achievement is that he affirmed that herein lies the freedom of the children of God.

Recently a young man came to me, a teacher from a neighboring district. He was baptized, he came to church to learn, he was asking about the Inquisition and other things. I said to him, "This is the simplest thing, we have criteria by which we can discern the most important from the peripheral." In the novel by Graham Greene, *The Power and The Glory*, this comes through very clearly in the conversation of the hero and the lieutenant who is escorting him to his punishment. The hero says to him "If in your ranks there are bad people then everything fails because for you everything depends on people. We, on the other hand, may have bad people, but in fact with us everything lives by something else." And he said directly, "our God fashions the sons of Abraham from stones and he can always find them," in order to demonstrate that i fact all this is not a human enterprise.

This is why I'm always amazed at the deliberations of many Western theologians who discuss the future of Christianity. They speak about it in the same terms, with the same mindset, as one would discuss the destiny of some kind of organization or party: How is it doing? Will it succeed or not? Will it have an audience for its ideas or not? Such conversations are absolutely mindless. If one were to place these gentlemen in the times of the Apostles, then what would they say? What kind of social conditions existed then! "The rebel is crucified!"—there is such a good poem of A. K. Tolstoy "Against the Current," where he says, "The rebel is crucified"—and that is all! Of course, now we don't much care, but at that time, many things came to the surface. Likewise, Leo H. Tolstoy used to call it a kind of a monastic squabble. Thus, to judge the Church purely on the basis of sociology is an entirely myopic undertaking. That is why we speak about her dual nature, about her theandric nature.

Here, we members of the Church are its instrument; but what happens with us is always a miracle. We are in no way a special interest club, although of course you and I have many things in common in life, character, and goals. Nevertheless, there is a certain mystery which will continue to unite us beyond this because, "where two or three are gathered in my name I am in the midst of them," and this will overcome our weaknesses. This is not a mystery which is formalized, and we receive authority; but we receive it conditionally, to the extent that, "whoever wishes to be first must be your servant." It must be said that this was even the case with the Old Testament Church.

When we begin to read history, we find perhaps a nation in revolt, or some unworthy rulers. All of this is not simple, the discussion is complex and intense. But as to the concept of Chief Pastor, then sociologically one must concede that it has great value. Certainly, it is more convenient when the Church's administration is separate from the State, when it has a certain autonomy, when it has a huge theological apparatus, and so forth, which gives it greater mobility. But this has its own dangers. And we must always discern what belongs to the Church of Christ , and what its extraneous aspects are.

8

A Conversation about Redemption

In the ancient world the problem of redemption was resolved rather simply because the ancient understanding of this concept was influenced by a specific juridical concept of the relationship between man and God. People functioned with this understanding in their daily lives. The dominant relationship was that of vassal to lord: the one who offended his master was obliged to give satisfaction. The understanding about honor in feudal times and later on was also closely tied to the idea of satisfaction. The offended side would demand from the vassal, or even an equal partner, that the offense would be satisfied by some action, and such ideas found their way to the theological level to the mystery of redemption.

At the end of the last century Patriarch Sergius spoke vehemently against this in his interesting book entitled, *The Doctrine of Redemption,* where he categorically refutes as inconsistent with the spirit of the New Testament this juridical idea that people need to find some sort of satisfaction for the offended God—failing which, Christ himself with His suffering satisfies the offended anger of God and thereby solves the juridical problem. In fact, in Sacred

Scripture the dominant symbols are of a different order; they are rather organic, biological, where the mystery of redemption is seen as a process of purification, transformation, joining man, grafting him to another, divine life.

In some way this is reminiscent of the work of a gardener who grafts a healthy organism onto a sick one in order to defeat the sickness; but the juridical understanding of the dogma of redemption and its various forms has to some degree been founded on the letter of Scripture, because even the very term redemption implies buying something, buying one's way out. Naturally, it appears juridical. This term was used in the ancient slave trade when someone released a person, bought him out of slavery. He thus made him a free man not by releasing him entirely from slavery, but by redeeming him for himself. This does not mean that initially the person was a slave of one person and then became the slave of another. No, he was indeed the slave of the first but once redeemed, purchased, he became the moral debtor of the other one, that is, he became a free man yet a moral debtor. There is still another important aspect of this term. In the symbolism of the Old Testament, this word "redemption" is encountered in connection with the problem and the theme of Exodus. God says: I purchased you and I made you my own. This means that the God of the chosen people predestined them for his purpose, saved them from evil, he didn't simply release them into the wilderness, but he made them his own, that is, the locus in which he would perform his acts, that field of battle, creative laboratory, center of the presence of highest divine powers which he establishes on earth.

The Apostle Peter repeats this idea in speaking to the Church as a chosen people, as God's holy elect. And when Moses says: "You will be a kingdom of priests and a holy people," what does he have in mind here? It is precisely this group of people which must serve God: the kingdom of priests, a holy people that is consecrated to him for service, here is the precise meaning. In this way God takes to himself those who are redeemed, purchased, chosen, from slavery for himself; and this model later is applied to the work of Christ who rescues people from the kingdom of evil and leads them to where they can become God's elect. This is what we find in Holy Scripture. A peculiar organism develops that lives by another principle. In it Christ becomes incarnate. This organism is the faithful themselves, the Church. He wants us to be his body. What does this mean, his body? The body is that which lives, acts, moves, shows activity. God's activity must come to life in us. This is the idea of the Apostle Paul, that the Church is the body of Christ, "You have the mind of Christ," he says. "It is no longer I who live, but Christ lives in me." This means that we are purchased by him, redeemed from slavery, liberated. This means that the mystery of redemption is first of all the mystery of liberation; secondly, this mystery unites us to God's holy elect where God is active; and thirdly, this is the mystery of bearing our burden.

Here we must move to the historical cosmic level. The universe is formed and develops along two principles: the universe evolves on the one hand according to the vision of God and on the other hand it is constantly penetrated by the elements which oppose this principle. I will formulate this notion with the following short statement: Blind is the one who does not see the harmony of the world, but equally blind is he who fails to see the disharmony of the very same world. If the harmony of the world proceeds from the highest vision of the Creator, if God sees it in the creation of the world from a point outside of time when he says that the world is extremely good (the Hebrew expression "tov meyod" which is hard to translate), then this is God's vision; but in the historical process there is still the clash of polarized forces, polarized within creation itself. The fact that there are forces which contradict God's own idea is a self-evident fact. These forces are always described in the Bible symbolically through images, a pictorial language: the raging sea as a symbol of chaos, the dragon who becomes a personification of this sea, the snake which tempts Adam, and so forth.

On the level of the physical world, let us refer to this as chaos, as a current carrying the world towards death, to a state of entropy . Thus, the history of creation, the genesis of the cosmos, becomes the history of conflict, the conflict between Chaos and Logos, God's wisdom which codifies his ideas in the world. Why do the dialectics of Heraclitus, the dialectics of Hegel, reveal opposition in the world? How did the Zoroastrian religion already intuit the conflict of light and darkness in the world? Because the world is bi-polar: one pole proceeds from the creative God while the other proceeds from the degenerative force in creation. Here we may ask, what is the root of this movement away from God, of this flight into nothingness? To describe this in rational terms means to make sense of it but to make sense of what is meaningless is impossible. It can only be described conditionally. Only poetry, only the fruits of artistic creativity, can provide for us a picture of this irrational drive towards nothingness; for example, the portraits of evil painted by Dostoevsky and Baudelaire show us that there is a tendency towards evil but that it is impossible to demonstrate this logically.

The flight into darkness. A more interesting attempt

to explain this came from Berdiaev, who based his approach on the teaching of Schelling and Jakob Boehme. This viewpoint proposed the following: freedom as an absolute potential, as an absolute possibility to go in any direction including into the abyss of non-being, does not depend on God because it exists as a reality not established by God. This is why, when God establishes the world, this polarity remains and in some way constantly poisons creation. But Berdiaev expresses himself through mythology as does Schelling, he is clearly using a mythological language. Jakob Boehme says that this "ungrund," this primitive, inexplicable, indescribable abyss in which the divinity exists and from which God comes forth as a personality, contains a certain mixture of evil and good. This is an intuition, a vision, a poetic interpretation, mythology, not something which can be rationally described.

The fact remains that in God's creation there are conflicting primordial powers as creative as the rest, but opposed to God and for some reason permitted by God. We can of course guess why. Creation is one entire whole, and in order to repel this anti-divine vector, this impulse towards darkness, creation must itself remain free. But essentially, creation *per se* does not contain freedom. Only the one who personalizes creation is free, and this one is man. But man appears after the conflict between Chaos and the Logos, after the birth of organizing structures, of the basic laws of elementary particles, at the formation of life which disintegrates but which relays its baton along to its descendants. At the creation of man, life already transmits its information further without a genetic code, simply transmits it.

I very much like the words of the German poet Novalis: "man is the Messiah of nature." Man is introduced into nature, man's spirit is joined with flesh in order to carry within each of his cells the sea of all living things and plants. We are after all a microcosm; we carry everything inside us; all creatures live within us and we are called to participate in the battle between Chaos and the Logos, entering into the Logos, into illumination. But man failed to accomplish this mission; and here God begins to act himself, through man. Not only the Divine "Information", Not only the creative Logos, but the Logos who becomes incarnate in man, begins to act in the world.

"In the beginning was the Logos and the Logos was with God, and the Logos became flesh"—this is what we read in John's Gospel. "Became flesh"—What does this mean? Became a man. In biblical language the word "flesh" means man. In this way the evolution of the world, if we can put it this way, is stimulated constantly by God; and in a particular way he stimulates it to the creation of the spiritual creature, man. And finally, when He himself enters the process of the world, assumes the evil of the world as His cross, He pushes this world further along towards the Kingdom of God. Christ takes upon Himself the suffering of the world. For the first time, God involves Himself in this battle, but He does so according to a divine principle. This divine principle is: constant humiliation, a kind of diminution of the Divine power before the face of creation, to give it the freedom of manifesting itself, the freedom to become what it is. And man enters a world in which he is forced to do battle, to fight with temptations and with the surrounding nature in which evil rules.

What is it that tempts man? He is tempted by the will to power. The will to power is the most serious impulse and the heaviest sin of man. Behind all social, political and cultural wars lies the will to power.

Freud was wrong in thinking that at the basis of everything is the libido, sex. Not at all. Millions of people have rejected sex, millions of people have rejected marriage, but no one has ever rejected power. We must always remember this. Human civilization is built on the fall, on original sin. It has preserved in itself this impulse to power which is why all magic is built precisely on the desire to rule over nature, as is our technological civilization. An entirely accurate account of all of human history could be written from the standpoint of the will to power, the lust for power.

If you analyze any significant event you will see the colossal role played by the thirst for power. The fact is that this impulse does not escape a person even in old age. A person can be totally disinterested in food, disinterested in a variety of life's pleasures, can even be barely mobile; yet this power will remain the last and only thing which brings him joy and happiness.

The fall—here was that first moment when the will to power became dominant in man. In biblical symbolism, and I emphasize this, the knowledge of good and evil does not mean an intellectual knowledge, but signifies, rather, control; for the word "daat" means a close relationship and is used in connection with a mastery over something, conjugal relations and other similar things. The expression "good and evil" is really an idiom, "tov-ve-ra;" this short term means good and evil and has nothing to do with moral categories since "tov" means pleasureful, enjoyable, wholesome, whereas "ra" means the unpleasant, poisonous—these are the two poles of creation, an expression which signifies simply all of creation as such, nature as such, world as such.

And when God introduces Himself into the current of human life, he finds for Himself a people who rejects his power, who says rather "Thy will be done". Who are

93

these people? This is Abraham, this is Moses (who incidentally does nothing according to his own will but only repents), these are the prophets. And finally it is Christ in his complete and perfect self-giving: "To do not my will but the will of the Father who sent me."

Why does the Church insist on the fact that Christ was an absolute and perfect man? Because without this everything loses its purpose. Christ was not only God incarnate for us but he was one of us, our human brother, our flesh and blood brother, part of the human race and on behalf of humanity he said to God, "Yes." Thanks to this mystery the world progressed further. Why did the Apostles say that Christ wanted neither praise nor recognition? He did not desire to claim for himself the name of God, but he humbled himself even to the form of a slave. Here in contrast to Adam who wanted to be like God, the Apostle describes Christ who declined everything, who took upon himself the fate of the accused, the accursed ones.

He was not a priest (take note, as one writer pointed out, that the only true priest was never actually a priest). He was not someone in authority, he belonged to no specific category and his royal lineage was strictly symbolic. He didn't study in any special academies, he lived as any average person, he sank to the very pit of life, he was spat upon by the crowd, he was judged by a civil religious court and finally, he was condemned as a blasphemer and a rebel—He took upon himself all the sufferings of the world, He made Himself a participant in these sufferings. In this way two worlds became united, the divine world and the world of suffering humanity and creation. God reclaimed the world; and carrying the cross, Christ in a certain sense continues to bear in himself all the ensuing development of mankind. He ascended, and this means that he permeated all aspects of the universe. We repeat these very important words in the Creed, "and sits at the right hand of the Father." We must reject an artificial conception of this sitting at the right hand of the Father. This clause means that Christ is there where God is, and God is everywhere.

In this way the God-man becomes the flesh of the world; and the flesh of the world, the universe, becomes the flesh of the God-man. He sanctifies all things. You see, the man Jesus who walks in the desert is not an isolated phantom in the cosmos but a being who is part of the biosphere, of the noosphere, part of nature. Connected with it, he eats, he drinks. At the same time, inasmuch as he is united with the oneness of the universe, through him the Divine becomes involved in its creation. For this reason the redemption becomes an act, a mystery which furthers the act of creation. There is nothing here of the notion of medieval satisfaction, of a juridical trade, substitution, game, or process. There is no legal process, but there is a process of the healing of mankind which is linked with the larger vision of creation.

If God heals matter, placing within it the forces of progression, if He heals that which is dead giving it the impulse towards life, if He heals the dying life, placing within it man who carries such spiritual and immortal information—finally He redeems the history of the world and of man by entering into it Himself. This indeed is the mystery of redemption of the human race and of the whole world, for the Apostle Paul gives these wonderful words: that the whole creation groans until now and suffers, waiting for the revelation of the sons of God; that is, all of nature finds itself in such a sickly state of imperfection and incompleteness, groaning and anticipating this day. Although Christ appeared for mankind, since He was incarnate in this world, sooner or later His redemption will permeate the whole universe. This is confirmed by the words of Holy Scripture: John the visionary saw not only the new man reborn and resurrected, reclaimed according to God's plan—but he saw a new Heaven and a new Earth, for the old had passed away. Here is the whole meaning; here in a few words, is the meaning of the Redemption, but again these are all words and symbols, so inadequate to convey the reality with clarity.

9

Encountering the Risen Christ

Seeing the Christ Child and hearing the word of the elder Simeon, the prophetess Anna proclaimed that salvation had come. Picture the word which embodies all this, a word familiar to us—the word "Meeting", or "Encounter". This word not only designates a parish feast[1], but it is the most important word of our inner life, because the most important moment for all of us is our Encounter with the Lord, our own personal Encounter with him. We have all come to Him and to the Church precisely because this Encounter has taken place. It could be that it takes place in every person: I am convinced that God knocks at the door of each of us, while often remaining anonymous. But man can reject Him, can turn his back on Him, can wish that the Encounter would not happen. And for us, who responded to this Encounter, however weak our voice, most precious is the fact that along our own path we have met You, Oh Lord. Like Anna we can testify that this has infinitely deepened our life, expanded our horizons, opened inexhaustible levels, given us the strength for struggle despite the difficulties on our path.

Nonetheless, our journey upwards has begun. For you fairly young people the upward path is not always clear, because you are as yet ascending in life's basic aspects, physically. But when a person reaches a critical point in life, he begins to descend physically. And when you experience this, you will know how precious the fact that the Gospel, the power of God's Spirit, the Encounter with Christ, gives us the possibility of always ascending to such an extent —that however we crawl, whatever zig-zags we make, however we trip up, however we fall back—still, we are growing. The natural, unspiritual man always perceives only loss and more loss, while we are always gaining. If I were offered a chance to return to my twenties I would be horrified because, recalling this time of my life, I would feel impoverished, robbed in relation to all that I have acquired since those days. To part with such treasure would indeed be hard. That's why for us this Encounter is always a stimulus, a movement, an invitation to ascend.

So, what can we say about the Encounter. This mystery is deeply connected with the mystery of the Resurrection of Christ. You remember that when the Apostle Paul was describing how Christ appeared to him, about an actual Encounter, as if he had struck an invisible obstacle and fell, how he compared that turning point of his life with the appearance of the risen Christ to the disciple during the days of the paschal feast. Here we must draw a most important conclusion—that for us any inner Encounter with him is an Encounter with the *Risen* Christ, that in fact the Resurrection was not simply an occurrence localized in time and space. It is not something which fixed Christ in time and space; no, this would be untrue. But for us this presence of Christ in time and space is valuable essentially because there is another aspect of his presence

ence which transcends time and space. If Christ could be compared to Socrates, then we would be left with only memories. But it isn't simply that he once existed, but that he remains to the end of the age. And the Resurrection is a most profound, mysterious, real, earth-shattering metamorphosis which transposed the Gospel events from the narrow sphere of transient history to a scale visible from any point on earth, in any century.

You and I can meet Christ, who is journeying from Bethany to Jerusalem, in our memory, in a text, in our imagination, in a movie, in a book. But with the Christ Who rose from the dead, our Encounter is an inner one, because this indeed is the voice of God, the eyes of God, the face of God, the correlation of the eternal with the temporal, the everlasting with the finite, the divine with the human. Recently I saw a film about Moses. A renowned director was trying figuratively to depict how Moses experienced his Encounter with God on Mount Sinai. There arises an amorphous, fiery, dusty spout looking like a fake volcano, and from this plume of sparks and flames we hear the voice: "I am your God."

An impersonal being, related to an impersonal cosmos, to the endlessness of the universe in all its directions (endless—meaning not only in space, but unfathomable to our imagination). And if we are truly to imagine the reality of the Creator, then I don't think one can express it better than Lomonosov. You remember what he was describing when he witnessed the colossal configuration of northern lights in the sky which appeared at that time, and what he thought at the coincidence of Venus and the sun. When he saw Venus and suddenly, though mistakenly, perceived that it had an atmosphere and was a world comparable to ours, he wrote a fascinating article describing the possibilities of human civilization there, of the spiritual problems connected with that life, about how the Good News of Christ might relate to that culture. He was always preoccupied with the problem, "Look, how great is the Creator!"

In reality, the enormity of nature, the vastness of the universe, does not and cannot squeeze into us, because we are people, we are smaller, yet at the same time we are immeasurably larger. And in order for that non-human, indescribable Something, which created the universe and still controls it, to become Someone capable of communicating with us—it must acquire our voice and our language. A factor here is that we are in the image and likeness of God, that within us, metaphorically and not in a direct sense, we carry a spark of the Spirit, we resemble him, it seems we are related to him, you see, and in this lies the whole purpose of our life. Here are the possibilities and conditions for that Encounter. This weak, helpless, suckling, erect creature, passionate and atavistic, is still capable of discerning the Divine. But in order for this capacity to function in us, God comes to us and places himself on a plane on which we can grasp him. This is the meaning of the Resurrection.

Christ arose so that His humanity and divinity would become for us a reality today, here, in the soul of each individual person. What do we mean by salvation, Savior? What does the word "salvation" mean? It means to come out of nothingness, from a delirious life of fantasy towards a real life. Man is amphibious, the man-amphibian is a being who by nature is called to live on two planes to inhabit two worlds. We are not spirits, but we are also not simply biological beings; we belong to another category. And this is not mere conjecture, ideas, ideologies rather, God reveals Himself, is diffused throughout, revealing Himself in nature, in human wisdom—in every thing. He revealed himself personally in Christ Jesus, who was initially localized in a particular place, in a particular slice of history, and then this localization erupted.

The Resurrection and the Ascension (in the given case they are one and the same) effectively ended the localization. And today for us, the Lord is here and now. This is why instead of saying, I am leaving you some written directives, He said: "I remain with you for all the days until the end of the age." This is what we are reading at this time: "I remain..." And this is a possibility for each of us, the basis of Christian experience. You see, such is the experience of an unsophisticated mysticism and of all religions: each has its own worth, all this is wonderful, all hands reaching towards heaven—these are miraculous hands, worthy of man's calling, because these are the hands of the creature, the image and the likeness of God, which strain towards their Prototype. But Christ is the hand which reaches downward, as we see on some ancient icons, the hand reaching towards us from out there. Everything is built on this—but the most profound Encounter with God can only be in Christ. Here lies the mystery of the Jesus Prayer. All the ancient meditations, which had to do with the repetition of certain texts, mantras, etc., responsive to nuances of the human psyche, extraordinary phenomena—are here subject to the name of Jesus. In order that this prayer would never become an aimless contemplation, something abstract, something faceless—at the center of our inner relation to God there is always the Lord Jesus. If this were not so, then all Christian mysticism would dissolve, becoming indistinguishable from Zen Bhuddism, and so forth. This is the reason why Christ says in Scripture, "I am the Alpha and the Omega, the beginning and the end."

If you want to find something real in Christianity, then

search for it only through the Risen Christ. Secondly, the Resurrection means victory. It means that God entered our human struggle, the great struggle of spirit against darkness, evil, oppression. He who was rejected, condemned, killed, humiliated, somehow focused all the misfortunes of the world in himself and triumphed over all of them.

In weakness, in crucifixion God revealed his power, and he reveals it still. I need to remind you that the Apostle Paul said: all of us need to experience the Resurrection, this special Encounter with God, in this life; but this is inseparable from crucifixion. He says (as in the epistle read at baptisms) that we are crucified with Christ, that with him we share sufferings common to us all, inner torments, external sorrows—each one has his own difficulties which he carries in life—if we understand them as participation in the sufferings of Christ, who suffers for the whole world, whose heart bleeds, because that heart contains all the hearts of the world. To die with him in order to rise with him. The Apostle endured this in a unique way, and the experience of such a dying is inexpressible. To talk about it is rather hard, more precisely, almost impossible. But each of us who finds himself in a critical situation, an illness, a tough condition, should remember that this condition can be sanctified; we can transform it into a cross. We always need to remember that next to Christ were two thieves, one simply suffered, while the other co-suffered with Christ and heard the words, "Today, you will be with me in Paradise."

This means that the Resurrection is not something that occurred once upon a time proving Christ's victory to the disciples, something which had its place two thousand years ago. The Encounters continued to happen, they always happened. Recall the important fact that the Apostle Paul saw Christ with his inner eye—Paul, a person who had not walked with Christ, who was alien to Him, who was not His personal disciple; this is the hope for the future path of all Christians. Paul said: "God deigned to reveal his Son to me." That God opens himself to us through his Son is a unique experience; this is the experience of the Resurrection. Then we find ourselves together with Mary Magdalene, who believed in Him; when each Pascha is for us this special day—and not necessarily the day of Pascha itself. Because there is no longer a day when the Lord who is present in the world is not our companion, waiting for us, knocking at the doors of our heart, "Lo, I stand at the door and knock." Here lies the meaning of the Resurrection, today's meaning, for this time, not for history, not for the past, but for this day. And the Lord himself said, "If I don't go away, then the Spirit will not come to you." If He would not leave the world as one who remains constrained locally and limited in space, then none of the subsequent events would have occurred, there would have in fact been no universal Church nor Christianity. He began to act regardless of human weaknesses, in spite of all historical circumstances, and He acts today again regardless of human weaknesses, in spite of historical circumstances. He will triumph always; and He has only begun His work, only begun, because His aim is the Transfiguration of the world, the Kingdom of God. We only need to anticipate this, to feel its coming. The Kingdom of God is what the Lord proclaimed to us, this reality is neither some futurology nor beyond the grave (although it is also one and the other); the Kingdom of God is what is in our inner existence when God reigns, rules, when He is at the center, when He sanctifies all our relations, when finally He becomes the foundation of all our actions, thoughts and feelings, when that which is weak and sinful moves to the periphery of our being while the Kingdom lies at the center. This is what we ought to pray for, strive for, what becomes essential for us; for in the Resurrection the Kingdom of God begins to grow and triumph.

So, here is all I wanted to share with you about this great mystery. One can utter many superficial words, but they can never convey the essential, and the most essential is *Encounter*. If each of you seriously contemplates his inner path, how God led you, the mystery of related events, the friendships, books, life situations, how all this occurred, you will readily understand that he continues to walk the earth, knock at innumerable hearts, and call people after him and to him. And he called each one of you, which is why each biography is in its own way a small part of Church history. It takes place in each one uniquely, yet with common traits, for there is one God, one faith, and one baptism.

[1]The Encounter or Meeting of the Lord in the Temple is one of th Twelve Major Feasts on the Orthodox calendar, celebrated Febru ary 2.

10

The Inner Step

Each one of us has his own personal and evident reasons for bearing a cumulative fatigue. It is hopeless to believe that by some means—let's say when vacation comes—things will radically change, since we have gone on vacations before, and have continued to rattle along just as hunched over as ever.

We are all young ; in any event, you are. Our era is amazing, in its own way fortunate, and I don't regret living in it. Nonetheless, its tempo is a heavy burden on Homo Sapiens. Particularly as we live in a large city. Stress presses upon us like a stone. But what is to be done?

There are all sorts of programs, self-improvement schemes, and so forth. I have examined these things practically and theoretically. I realized that only someone with ample free time can engage in these activities, which in themselves are not at all bad. We may not know all the factors that affect us. We know, for instance, what percent is genetically inherited, what percent is the result of conflicts at work and at home—in general things are tough. And our natural forces of regeneration, recreation, function rather weakly or not at all. This is why I want to remind you of what you know quite well without my saying so—that there are supernatural paths. Only through the force of the spirit can we finally acquire additional strength, can we conquer our spiritual flabbiness, our spiritual weakness. For this we don't particularly need any special methods of concentration as in those methodical self-improvement exercises; what we need—and I will simply remind you of commonly-known facts—is no less than six to ten minutes a day (I am now speaking of minimums) for prayer, in any form. If you are simply reading prayers, then just read them and do not give any less time to reading the Gospel, and in general Holy Scripture. So too, the Eucharist and common worship are necessary. Four things. This is not theory, it is tested practice.

Many who approach me with this common ailment of ours then say: "But I didn't follow this plan." At that point I don't know what to tell them. It's like a doctor saying to a patient, "You have a diseased liver, you can't eat fatty or salty things," while the patient returns saying, "Doctor, each day I consume a heap of lard and really enjoy herring." The doctor throws up his arms in frustration.

There are particular methods which produce specific results. There is a practical discipline which has more than a two-thousand year history.

But it is important to balance all four activities. It's useful to remember the following analogy: if you remove one of four table legs, the table falters; remove the second, and it falls. All the same, we need to remember that the gift of God, the grace and blessing of God, is not some kind of panacea or medicine, for in that case our egotism, our personal demands on God, would take first place. We don't desire to become something for him, yet we want him to become Something for us, useful for some purpose. With this attitude, things deteriorate.

The true approach requires a great inner step. In one of his tragedies Byron describes a flood. A man stands on a cliff and recites a monologue—he has such confidence in God that, even if everything drowns, he will still die full of hope. It is expressed well. If we don't have any guarantees about immortality, except that there is the will of God which directs all things, we know not how, and we find meaning only in the knowledge that it does so, and that in the flood we have meaning only through our connection to God, then for us this mystery is in the forefront; it guides us. And it isn't the case that, having a headache, I simply say a prayer for it to vanish. It may indeed happen that it does vanish, but that isn't the main goal. I began by saying how a proper method is important, how very necessary, but I need to modify this idea: such an egocentric utilitarian approach cannot be entirely right. We need to find still something else, to seek not only for ourselves. But this is a further step. One more thing: we have three forms of prayer, supplicatory (our favorite), repentance, and thanksgiving. Supplicatory prayer is blessed and commanded. And in the Our Father we have supplication. But notice that the Our Father begins not with a petition, but with something else —acceptance, agreement: "Thy will be done," "Thy kingdom come." And only later does the prayer say, "Give us this day our daily bread." You see, here is an inner liberation. We are not free, and we need to begin by being liberated from everything, straightening our spiritual "shoulders", hunched under a burden. I don't remember who said that if we observed half the Sermon on the Mount all our complexes would vanish. This is really so. Something constantly gnaws at us. Constantly gnaws. What's more, we become neurotics: I must do this, I must do that, I must do everything. Then the concern turns from something benign into a nuisance, because it becomes a nagging idea, a burdensome background of preoccupations. Here, remember that we are mortal, that life is short, and that our Lord said: "Don't worry about what to eat and drink tomorrow." He said it precisely in this sense. Our eyes sense fear, and our hands act. They act on impulse. Even if you make a plan for the future, it must be a free-hand sketch, and not some kind of binding thing which makes you a slave.

We are free and we are fortunate, despite those weaknesses which cripple us. Because we commune with the mystery of God's grace, many awesome and wonderful things are revealed to us. Besides this, we have brothers and sisters, we have them here, in the temple, throughout the city, throughout the whole earth. We are included in the divine eternal. And one more extraordinary thing: through the divine prism we are capable of examining everything, scientific formulas, any phenomena. This morning I turned on the television and saw an eight-legged creature—a divine sight, simply a divine sight! And this for only a few seconds. Unfortunately the film ended quickly, but it brought me to a state of complete wonder. And any thing can provoke in us delight. We should not lose the capacity to look at things in a fresh way, at our loved ones, the surrounding world, and try to go easy on the turns, live more lightly; learn how to push aside, when necessary, our maddening demands; rise above them and become willing pilgrims. We are, after all, pilgrims. We are simply guests here, visitors. The Apostle Paul says that we are all pilgrims on the earth, merely guests and visitors. In one apocryphal gospel the Lord Jesus says that the world is a bridge. Well, isn't a bridge for crossing over?

We speak about a Father, who is in heaven, but what is a Father? He is our relative, the One most closely related to us. And what is the meaning of "in Heaven"? On another level of existence, Heaven is our fatherland. By "fatherland" I don't have in mind an earthly birthplace or some sort of emotional bond, I mean something entirely different. You can have an emotional connection to your street, house, mother tongue, town, country. This is a natural quality of man. But there is something else which we call fatherland. This is hard to convey, but Lermontov made an attempt in his famous poem about an angel singing while carrying a soul to earth when it was due to be born, and this soul always retained the sounds of the angel's song. This is only an image, yet a very profound one, because we do have another birthplace. We are linked with something of the spiritual world, and that is why we are guests, at times uncomfortable in this world; and in part this is at it should be, for the world is filled with coarse matter, the world lies in evil. We collide with it, and it injures us. More importantly, we need to appeal to the Spirit, and the Spirit comes especially when we are together. That is why we gather in the temple, that is why we pray together as much as we are able.

Thus, the paschal days are coming to a close, this season is ending, and we are somehow experiencing it all anew. And again the risen Lord comes to us, as in Emmaus, when He came to the disciples. He says, "Peace be with you!" "Peace be with you," is not simply an ancient greeting. Of course He greeted them, but into this greeting he put something very profound. In the ancient Hebrew the word "shalom" ("peace") means not only "no war," but a particular state of grace, peace of soul, closeness to God, and it is this peace that we ask of Him. Peace with God, peace among each other. Let us pray this way, so that we may understand that He is still with us. And the word of God will be with us and we will carry it home, and it will live in us. Finally, let us live brightly and in hope. We are the fortunate who make no use of their fortune and we are the rich who neither dispose of their wealth nor use it for themselves. So, today, let us wash away everything, all our hurts, our sorrows, our worries and expectations, our sins, our burdens. And let us ask that God would strengthen us. This is the most important thing. And now, let us pray:

Lord Jesus Christ!

In this evening hour, in this city,
Where Your blessing rests,
amidst all sufferings and sins and troubles,
You, Who suffered
and assumed all the ills of mankind,
because You loved us,
You, Who have come here,
remain with us.

Lord, You bore the Cross.
Teach us to carry sufferings and burdens
for the sake of our loved ones.

Lord Jesus Christ,
You see our wounds and our weaknesses.
Pour strength into us, make us firm, virile,
worthy witnesses of Your Divine Gospel.

Lord Jesus Christ,
Grant us in those days which You assign us,